The Color Of Our Souls

How Multigenerational Experiences Impact Our Lives

The Color of Our Souls
How Multigenerational Experiences Impact Our Lives

The Color of Our Souls
How Multigenerational Experiences
Impact Our Lives

ISBN: 13: 979-8553750190
IMPRINT: Indie Publishing

Printed in the United States of America
10 9 8 7 6 5 4 3 2 1

THE COLOR OF OUR SOULS
How Multigenerational Experiences Impact Our Lives

by
Brian C. McGuire
Towson University

FAR-LEFT PUBLICATIONS

Brian C. McGuire

The Color of Our Souls
How Multigenerational Experiences Impact Our Lives

Brian C. McGuire was born in Baltimore, Maryland on May 31, 1970. He spent thirteen years serving in the United States Armed Forces. He received a Bachelor of Science from Towson University. His areas of research interests include the mental terrain of Community Psychology: A field of Human Services that places special emphasis on problems associated with urban groups and how they adapt under low socioeconomic conditions during childhood, adolescence, and throughout the course of adult development and aging, and sociocultural influences (including theoretical concepts pertaining to how various dimensions of culture influence stress and coping). Brian is also the author of these exceptional indie reference books: The Ignoble Paradox of Man and The Great Divide: The Social and Cultural Context of Inequality.

The Color of Our Souls

TABLE OF CONTENTS

Dedication

The Color of Our Souls is dedicated to Blacks across this great nation, many of whom are in need of healing. I'm not just referring to healing in the sense of rectifying something that causes discord and animosity, which the book is partly about. Nor is the book solely about spiritual healing. In fact, it is a curative literature piece written with the effect of healing or improving serious disagreements that disrupts good relationships. Unless we can heal the rift that exists between us, there is little chance of recovering spiritually or emotionally. Might this book rid us of the wrong, evil, or painful affliction that causes many of us to hemorrhage spiritually and emotionally! Let it restore our injuries naturally and bring our understanding to good mental health.

Acknowledgements

I'd like to thank all those who offered help in the development of this book. It was one of my greatest challenges. Without their help and encouragement, this book would have not come to fruition. I've made serious and sincere efforts to educate the public on the plight and predicament of Blacks in America. But, the people I acknowledge have made my job, that is to say, writing this book, that much easier.

I am deeply indebted to Yvonne M. Drake for her continued love and support throughout the writing process of this book.

I am especially grateful to Anita L. Opher. Her editorial genius and continued dedication in the development of this book is invaluable.

I'd also like to thank Kendra for her encouragement, which inspired my confidence and will to continue in the writing process of this book.

I'd like to give a personal thank you to Shamya Trent. Her artistic skills in advising me in the creation of the book cover and chapter sections are invaluable. Her contributions on sections I wrote about the LGBTQIA community are bar none. Without her knowledge and encouragement, this book would be impossible to complete.

And finally, special thanks go out to Tameika Trent. Her resourcefulness in the marketing and promotion of this book has been truly a great contribution.

I appreciate them all.

Prologue
On The Color of Our Souls

The transatlantic slave trade transported enslaved Africans to the Americas from the 14th to the 19th century. Called middle passage, it was the second segment of the global slave trade in which 10 to 12 million Africans were forcibly transported across the Atlantic Ocean to the Americas as chattel. As part of the trade, ships departed European markets with arms, textiles, and wine shipped to Africa. The enslaved were shipped from Africa to the Americas; and, sugar and coffee were shipped from the Americas to Europe.

The first passage was the transportation of the enslaved to African ports where they would be loaded onto slave ships. The storage spaces where they were housed were only 18 to 24 inches in height. Africans stayed confined in those spaces throughout the three month voyage. It is where many of them "slept, wept, ate, defecated, urinated, regurgitated, menstruated, gave birth, and died." That was the condition in which they were kept.

Final passage was the third segment of the journey, ranging from American ports, such as New York, Jamestown, Virginia and Charleston, South Carolina to trade markets and other destinations where enslaved Africans would be sold as chattel into US slavery.

McGuire (in press)

After slavery, Blacks were the only people made to endure segregation, eugenics, prejudice, and discrimination well into the new millennium. The science behind this reasoning was to keep them deprived of their humanity. It is our humanity that helps us relate to others and to function in the real world.

How did the system of slavery work to help explain our behavior in everyday conversations? History suggests there hasn't been any accountability or reconciliation for Blacks to progress as a people. Yet, Blacks show remarkable adaptiveness, resilience, and responsibility as they continue to endure at the hands of their oppressors.

"We must widen our circle of compassion to embrace all living creatures" if we are to develop our humanity. In this prologue, On the Color of Our Souls, we will explain what led to the development of this book. You will see in this passage and throughout the book, it is a necessary way of understanding who we are as a whole.

The Color of Our Souls was inspired by the lectures of Dr. Joy DeGruy and, in part, from professional writings of the eminent Negro scholar W. E. B. Du Bois. In his book, The Souls of Black Folk, Du Bois recognized, immediately, that the color line was a twentieth century problem. His book was written to address the continued problem of White supremacy in America. He spoke to the hesitance of White people's humanity and their lack of compassion shown toward Black folk. In fact, his comments suggested a disconnection in their compassion, a cognitive disconnect thoroughly discussed in Dr. DeGruy's public lectures on Post Traumatic Slave Syndrome: America's Legacy of Enduring Injury and Healing.

Dr. DeGruy's lectures on Post Traumatic Slave Syndrome were uplifting and gave the audience a life-affirming message. And, at the same time, I was left feeling exhilarated. I finally found someone who understood how multigenerational trauma impacted the lives of Black folk. In fact, her work could only be explained as seminary as she hit the nail on the proverbial head.

Dr. DeGruy or, simply, Joy, as she likes to be called, focused on cognitive dissociation surrounding the issue of race. Her investigation reported on the impact of oppression, slavery, and the system of segregation that ensued, resulting in multigenerational adaptive behaviors of which some were positive, reflecting resiliency while others inherently negative thus detrimental and destructive.

When investigating into the pathology of race, she noticed it tended to cause hostility among White people. In fact, she noticed there was a cognitive disconnection between their words and their actions. Her observations left me in awe.

Dr. DeGruy believed White people suffered from cognitive dissonance. I thought to myself, how thought-provoking and humbling. Her field work and research were the missing links needed to connect two worldviews. Her review of American scholarship on the topic highlighted a cognitive disconnection between two separate and distinct cultural systems, one inherently White and the other was penitently Black.

DeGruy realized Black people adapted under incredible circumstances. And that many White people felt

Blacks refused to overcome centuries of prolonged adversity. But, she understood they never had a chance to heal. She knew they wanted to be socially accepted in order to feel included. But, the wanting was part of their trauma. She also understood the problem of America and its legacy of enduring injury and healing. That Black people were never allowed to heal (i.e., recover spiritually or emotionally) was the difference between achieving true acceptance and existing under the illusion of inclusion.

Now, I understood her when she began talking about Black people never having the opportunity to heal. This concept struck a chord with me. There's never been mental health support, economic recovery assistance, or federal relief aid given in goodwill of Black suffering. The will of Blacks had been suppressed so much that they looked for acceptance through White peer approval. This concept was what DeGruy meant by post traumatic slave syndrome.

The Black bourgeoisie (Black middleclass) began under the illusion of inclusion. The Black middleclass, also a byproduct of the White Establishment, was nothing more than sycophants acting obsequiously toward the federal government. The government gave college educated Black people jobs and opportunities to put poor Black people under the illusion they could actually be included into mainstream society given an education.

But their idea of inclusion was to first deindustrialize urban cities. First, the government removed manufacturing plants, automobile factories, and industrial warehouses from urban cities. Next, high school trade programs were removed. And then, government officials told poor Black people that in order for them to benefit from social integration, they had to educate themselves. The idea was once they became educated, Black people would seek gainful employment to become a part of the cultural mainstream.

The problem for them was the same as it is today. Blacks have to take their degrees into White sectors of the community. These degrees, often obtained from historically Black colleges and universities (HBCUs) do not have the same value as their White counterparts, many of whom are affluent. Community-based businesses are obligated to hire within the community, first. Therefore, degrees obtained by Blacks lose value when used outside of their community. Extrinsically, their degrees lose value in the job market. So, having degrees, even degrees obtained from Ivy League colleges and universities, are worthless. Although important opportunities open for some, millions of college educated Black folk more than often find themselves unemployed. Many more believe they can make it on the basis of merit. Others end up working mediocre jobs in fast food industries as clerks and managers, left under the illusion of inclusion.

Even before the 1970's, segregation wore on the mindset of Black folk. During the Civil Rights movement, the government introduced the idea of social integration. Many Blacks felt they would never be accepted on the basis of merit. That they needed White peer approval or endorsements from Whites in order for their existence to feel validated. So, many gave up their businesses and lifestyles for an opportunity to be socially integrated. Black folk have been under the illusion of inclusion ever since.

The point is Blacks had been taught they were the White man's burden. That if they pulled themselves up by their bootstraps and became educated, they would not be forced to rely on the White man for money or support. This notion is what began the Black bourgeoisie. In other words… post traumatic slave syndrome.

The Color of Our Souls is my third attempt to raise awareness about how multigenerational experiences impact our lives here in America. It was written to open a dialogue, specifically, between Whites and Blacks. Now, I'll be the first to acknowledge my personal limitations in undertaking this latest endeavor. Although I am very confident about the information presented, any sophomoric attempts to competently address the topic are due to a cognitive disconnection that exists among and between identity groups here in America. This state of emotional isolation and disinterest may be voluntary or involuntary. But, the result is a complete lack of resources readily available on the topic.

The ability of these dynamic duos, DeGruy and Du Bois, called into question, my fundamental purpose in life: to speak out against all forms of inequality and to undermine the authority and legitimacy of White supremacy. I found Du Bois' approach to understanding the system of segregation intellectually profound. DeGruy's groundbreaking research on trauma, historical trauma, and multigenerational trauma was heart-wrenching and revealing. At the same time, her research was innovative and pioneering. Both scholars had a profound impact on my undertaking of this latest endeavor.

The title, The Color of Our Souls, is a spin-off from W. E. B. Du Bois' book The Souls of Black Folk. However, that's where it ends. My book was not intended to be a professional essay. Nor do I care to mimic the flare and fluency of creative writing Du Bois so eloquently accomplished in his writings. Instead, this book was written, largely, from a scientific perspective.

In my approach to this topic, I address the characteristic spirit of Black folk, most of who continue to endure in the face of overwhelming stress and oppression. Both DeGruy and Du Bois were important pioneers in the development of theoretical ideas on racism. They also conducted research on how White supremacy influenced stress and coping. That's just another way of saying the color line is a continuing problem even in twenty-first century America.

The color line or, today, racial identity lines are a multigenerational problem. The topic of racial identity lines was broadened in order to include the trauma of racism (1936). Racism is a significant source of emotional abuse and trauma for Black people. Not only does its impact have negative consequences on them, it has less visible negative consequences on society as a whole. In addition, a small minority of researchers were working to incorporate racism as a psychosocial stressor. If accepted, it would be featured as a syndrome in the Diagnostic and Statistical Manual for Mental Disorders (DSM).

Dr. DeGruy said the problem with reporting on multigenerational trauma is once you label it a disorder, the American Psychological Association (APA) will try to record it in the DSM. Afterward, they will try to create a pill for it. And, you cannot create a pill for post traumatic slave syndrome. Again, the problem with multigenerational adaptive behaviors is you cannot correct it through the use of medication.

Understand what a profound impact her lectures had on me. I looked at the historical effects of racism, racism in contemporary America, and often wondered but never looked at how multigenerational experiences shaped the color of our souls. I even duped myself into believing I understood all it entailed. And with the title sounding simple or straightforward enough, writing on this topic was not suppose to be hard or daunting for me.

Truth of the matter is it took a great deal of time for me to gain a good understanding of the topic. The title was more elusive than it sounded. In order for me to put my best effort into it, I had to explore many avenues. There were many ways I could have addressed it. And, I addressed it from every angle imaginable. My academic, professional, and personal skills were on deck, ready for use in the development of this book.

When I wrote this book, I never truly understood if this was a vice or virtue. There are a few chapters dedicated to explaining the title and topic. I dedicated seven chapters to the development of this book. There are two hundred pages committed to reading. Chapters are standard length for a reference book. Each chapter is self-contained. Thus, chapters can be read, randomly. But, if you are unfamiliar with the title and or topic, it would benefit you to finish reading the prologue, then the introduction, and finally, chapter one. These I deemed necessary in order for the reader to ascertain some understanding of the information presented. After chapter one, it can be read at random.

The information presented in this book is multi-faceted. Some of the information is inherently sociology, other parts draw from psychology, and still, much of this book involves sociocultural material both from my professional and personal experiences. The very purpose for writing this book was to educate or inform the public of continuing problems that exist between two separate and distinct cultural systems.

The color scheme for this book cover is symbolic of the color of sour souls. The multilayered blue waves are symbolic of nobility and loyalty as Black people have shown under the most adverse circumstances. The dark blue lines outlining the blue waves represent Black people's ties to humanity as they struggle to develop the qualities considered to be characteristic of humans. And the white background is characteristic of human souls as taught in fairy tales based in European mythology.

My goal is to raise awareness of and increase cultural literacy on how well Black people endure historical problems perpetuated by White supremacy. The amount of pages is characteristic of reference books. The Color of Our

Souls: How Multigenerational Experiences Impact Our Lives will prove to be a formidable read.

Segregation, state-sponsored violence, and antiblack racism continue to rank among society's most enduring and disabling problems. As violence by Whites against Blacks increase considerably, we have to recognize their situation. The fact is Black people continue to be subjugated under the most adverse conditions. Such problems will only end when White people recognize or acknowledge their role in its development. All other racial and ethnic groups fall into categories of either majority or minority. These groups—once society understands racism is no longer acceptable—will begin to make sense of it and adapt or cohere.

In this prologue, we gave a synopsis as to what inspired the creation of this book. In the introduction, we will explore important arguments that reveal its nature, giving way to a cascade of fascinating events that underlie the qualities considered to be characteristic of humans as a whole.

Introduction
The Color of Our Souls

In the 16 century, the state of Virginia introduced slave codes. Under this new system of oppression, indentured servants, specifically Black males, would enter into a period of servitude indefinitely. A clause introduced into the slave codes was antimiscegenation laws. These laws were among the earliest legislation passed as a deterrent against the admixing and potential rebellion of racial groups.

By 1619, in Jamestown, Virginia, indentured servitude was officially introduced as a system of chattel slavery. After the United States won its independence from England (1776), winning their rights to continue slavery, the newly formed Republic was eager to bring slavery under new colonial control. In 1789, Pennsylvania lawmakers introduced a piece of legislation called Criminal Codes and Penal Institution of Colonial Pennsylvania. One and only one concession was made for enslaved Blacks: The Three-Fifths Compromise:

> It was a resolution that would count three out of every five slaves as human when determining a state's total population. It was created for the purpose of legislative and taxation representation.

The preCivil War era began the period of segregation and, eventually, a reexamination of the slave codes. Called the black codes, many of the new codes were reassigned to include free Blacks. What many of today's people fail to understand is that the black codes officially began with the development of the first five slave-free states (1809).

Just after the Civil War, during the period of reconstruction (1866 – 1877), Congress declared all Blacks were US citizens:

> The Civil Rights Act of 1866 declared all male persons born in the United States to be citizens, without distinction of race or color, or previous condition of slavery or involuntary servitude.

Around the time segregation became federal law, and backed by institutional power, former Confederate General Nathan Bedford Forrest and his followers began an eleven year killing spree in Tennessee that led to the mass extermination of countless Blacks. And so began the trauma of racism.

McGuire (in press)

We are in thrall by the very nature of man. Humanity has been shattered by oppression and killing. Appalling crimes are committed against people regardless of race, color, or creed. The very nature of man has been shaped by traditions and colored by laws. And every shade of color further deprives him of his humanity. Yet, through the exploitation, oppression, and humiliation of it all, Black people remain on the humane side of humanity.

Throughout history, no other group of people endured adversity under the inhumane conditions set forth by the human race. Contrary to popular belief, Blacks are the only people on the planet who endured great cruelty at the expense of humanity. Now, that's not to say other races never endured oppression, slavery, or indentured servitude.

Europe was once known for committing unspeakable acts of great cruelty against its own people. They tortured their men, burned their women alive, and beat their children out of boredom. Hell, their brutal nature was accurately portrayed in a story given by Old Norse mythology. Vakyries—a host of female figures who choose those who may live in battle and those who will die—take their chosen to the afterlife, a place called Hall of the Slain, Valhalla, which is ruled over by the God Odin.

Many people believe aggression is the deepest and truest nature of humans. No society ever prospered without showing some level of aggression. America no longer hides behind the fact it's an imperialist empire. In fact, as President, Barrack Obama was given an international mandate, effectively authorizing him to carry out imperial policies that would once again make Africa safe for Western imperialists to exploit its resources. It was carried out under the military defense program USAfricom, a joint operations center at US Africa Command headquarters in Stuttgart, Germany.

Since USAfricom, the Ghanaian government authorized the United States to build the world's largest military base on its soil. Conspiracy theorists believe many of the bases being built in Africa are located geographically close to places with high levels of mineral reserves. Many feel it is a strategic plan to ensure Africa cannot defend itself if ever the people were to decide to fight back against Western imperialism. But, I digress.

The Characteristic Spirit of Black Folk

Now, there is evidence that supports the claim Blacks are a spiritual people. The church serves as testimony. When Dylann Storm Roof, a White supremacist, was convicted of killing nine Black church members, it was their congregation who forgave him. When a Dallas jury found former police Officer Amber Guyger guilty of murder for fatally shooting her neighbor Botham Jean, not only did Botham's family embraced Guyger in forgiveness, the Judge, a Black woman, came down off of her bench to openly embraced her, gave Guyger a Bible, and then brushed her hair in comfort. Black humanity runs deep in the prophetic traditions of the church.

The Black church has always been a staple in the Black community. It has long since been accredited with lifting the spirits of Black folk. Its intent was to awaken religious fervor in those who attended. The church has been a part of the Black community, dating back to the days of indentured servitude. It was discovered, at that time, the church could provide sanctuary to Africans who were often persecuted by their oppressors. Later Africans found satisfaction in the church as they learned it could be used as a substitution for village-based religion and tribal activities brought from Africa.

In fact, many of their concerns were taken up by the church. From the fight against slavery and wars waged by the Ku Klux Klan, to the induction of segregation in the antebellum South, their efforts were resolved through the sanctity of the church. The Civil Rights movement and the idea of integration were also fought through the efforts of the church. That's why church has always been an important influence in the lives of Black folk. It has become the major influence in their efforts to cope with stress and oppression. And, as a result, they learned to value religion above all else.

For a people to be subjected to excessive suffering, especially over prolonged periods of time, is bewildering enough. But to have them suffer to no end is wicked or immoral. Who would have thought that a people, sentient beings, could be wicked or malicious enough to oppress others for generations. It is only through the generosity of spirit that Black folk remain a compassionate and caring people. In spite of the wicked or immoral nature of man, Black people continue to overcome in the most courageous ways.

The effort to overcome did not begin in the new millennium. Nor did it happen in the aftermath or aftereffects of slavery. Truth of the matter is its human nature for people to overcome their circumstances. Despite being oppressed for two hundred fifty years in England, two hundred forty-six plus years in the Americas and, roughly, the same amount of involuntary servitude endured throughout Europe, Black people struggled successfully against oppression.

What other people have the capacity to tolerate, accommodate, or forgive their oppressors? Dare we wonder as no other group of people on this planet has the audacity to forgive their oppressors? Black people are a magnificent people. They are benevolent. They are the longest enduring people on earth. And why is that? Their humanity prevents them from being inhumane. We should celebrate the richness of their existence as an example to us all.

An Extraordinary People

Blacks are an extraordinary people. And, they deserve respect. Yet, their extraordinary circumstances have been bastardized by the very people we considered to possess high ideals or have strong morals and values. Dominant society devalued Black people by declaring them inferior. Dr. DeGruy would say they were removing the discomfort or dissonance from their existence: the first step in the process of subjugating a people. State-sanctioned violence and antiblack racism by law enforcement serves as testimony.

The Bell Curve, published in 1994, was written to prove the inferiority of Blacks. The book remains highly controversial, especially where the authors purported con-nections between race and intelligence. Arthur Robert Jensen (August 24, 1923 – October 22, 2012) was an American psychologist who spent his lifetime writing about the inferiority of Black people. Jensen was highly controversial due to his conclusions regarding the causes of race-based differences in intelligence. Many more people from dominant society supported White supremacy in that way.

Black people have an intellectual energy or intensity that connects them to a standard of moral courage, compassion, and commitment. They have the good judg-ment and sensitivity needed to avoid upsetting others. We praise them for their acceptance of generosity and thought-fulness. Although they continue to experience serious mal-treatment at the hands of their oppressors, Black people always show empathy and concern for folk from every walk of life. Yet today, they continue to endure inequality more than any identity group on earth.

They mourned with their oppressors when President John F. Kennedy was assassinated. They wept for British Royal Princess Dianna. When the US military issued drone strikes, killing hundreds of innocent souls in the Middle East, they protested. And, they prayed for answers while the world watched Notre-Dame de Paris cathedral in Paris burned down to the ground. Even before the thirteen British colonies formed a more perfect union, and indentured servitude meant serving a master or employer for a specified period of time, their humanity would only allow Black people to exist in a peaceful way with their oppressors. Thus, they are the souls of discretion.

The Nature of White Folk

Dominant White society is imbued with an emotive or exaggerated sense of dignity. Yet, I've looked into the hearts and minds of its members and found their humanity lacked soul. Many are often unconcerned for the sufferings or misfortunes of others. Slavery, Jim Crow segregation, eugenics, prejudice, bigotry, and discrimination left many apathetic toward the health and wellness of Black, Brown, and poor people. Their inability to display normal, passionate human feelings toward others or to respond emotionally against acts of inhumanity documented how well-adjusted they've become to indifference. And while poor and vulnerable people were continuously being exploited by dominant society, politicians promised them their dignities in return for their political rivals' defeat.

Dominant society always feared that Black people would impose the same exclusionary policy of racial inequality on Whites they imposed on Black people throughout their intellectual history. Yet, since the end of chattel slavery (1865), Blacks strived only to coexist with their oppressors.

During the Reconstruction Era (1866-1877), Whites formed secret societies with the goal of keeping Black people segregated, especially by enforcing separate housing, separate communities, and other, more drastic measures, usually by way of intimidation and murder. Discrimination against Black people by enforcing separate and unequal laws, formally called the slave codes, continued to describe the nature of their humanity. Although dominant society is now alarmed by a sense of oppression, their existence demonstrates an inability or unwillingness to become involved in the health and wellness of poor and vulnerable people.

Dominant society is a slave to western traditions. Its members follow a set of principles that view existing forms of society as worthy of preservation. They support a political philosophy based on gradual rather than abrupt change and work to preserve the status quo. Called Republicans, they share beliefs and practices that place their success at a particular place, class, or time in which their political philosophies were more important than others.

Beyond tradition, its members follow a body of doctrines that are viewed as a set of precedents and often accepted without written evidence. Handed down from generation-to-generation, their long-established customs are thought to be concerned with the ultimate perfectibility of man. Though technically perfect, their traditions lack the spiritual growth or emotional depth and sensitivity requisite for healthy intergroup relations.

The sad fact of it all is prolonged cruelty of oppression impacts their psyche. In order to deal with the impact of stress and coping, White people remove dissonance from the cognitive dimensions of their minds. In fact, they lost the ability to feel compassion and empathy for people they considered inferior. They reasoned from great philosophers like Aristotle who believed some people were destined to become slaves while others were destined to be rulers. Aristotle believed slavery was an act of nature. And that by a peculiar act of God, Black people were appropriate or suitable to serve as a laborious class, indefinitely. As a result of their reasoning, dominant society developed what could only be described as a blackened heart.

A Test of Endurance

Due to people who took on the bigoted philosophies of earlier scholars, Black people were never given the opportunity to heal. In fact, Blacks were stripped of their history and self-worth to ensure they would not experience cognitive dissonance. Not only were they deprived of their history and self-worth, they experienced severe emotional shock or distress, resulting in long-lasting psychological trauma.

They endured two hundred forty-six years of chattel slavery, at least one hundred years of segregation, two periods of eugenics, racism and White supremacy, prejudice, discrimination, and bigotry. And, through all of the shock or trauma, they never once received financial help or opportunity to restore their mental health. Yet, Black people show remarkable resilience and adaptation in the face of overwhelming stress and oppression. In that way, they became pinnacles of Modern-day miracles. In fact, they should be praised for their standards of humanity and dignity. Thus, the wickedness or immorality of oppression shapes the color of their souls.

The Nature of Black People
and their Circumstances

We criticize Blacks for their marginality. Most Black people are adversely affected by their circumstances. Unfortunately, the situation surrounding it is often controlled by chronic life conditions. These conditions impose considerable stress on Blacks and their families.

Inadequate housing, dangerous neighborhoods, burdensome responsibilities, economic uncertainties, and other chronic life conditions are potent stressors that adversely affect their circumstances.

Fortunately, their circumstances do not dictate who they are. If that were true, they'd be victims of their circumstances. Nor are they the total sum of their experiences. Although, a large part of who they are is shaped and colored by experiences that impact their lives.

All humans are endowed with the ability to change their circumstances. There are endless accounts of rags to riches stories that serve as testimonials. Many rise from poverty to wealth and, in some cases, from absolute obscurity to heights of fame, fortune, and celebrity. Samuel L. Jackson, a Black American actor and movie producer, was recorded as the highest-grossing actor of all times. But his success did not come overnight. Samuel L. struggled with chemical dependency most of his life. It wasn't until he cleaned up his act that he won his claim to frame. He was later awarded an Oscar for being the hardest working person in Hollywood showbiz. But, at other times, their circumstances changed instantly.

Jennifer Hudson and Fantasia were two of the most soulful singers in American entertainment. They both became overnight sensations after performing on the hit television series American Idol. Fantasia's style of singing was heartfelt and spiritual. Friends and family said she was an old soul. Fantasia attributed her success to the trials and tribulations of a struggling Black woman. Jennifer Hudson attributed her success to being persistent and persevering in the face of adversity. Both gave praises to God almighty. Similarly, Tyler Perry, a man who once lived in his car, now owns a movie studio larger than Paramount and Hollywood studios. Today, Tyler Perry owns Tyler Perry studios in Atlanta, Georgia. At other times, success is a slow mediocre rise to the top.

Octavia Spencer is a classic example. Octavia Lenora Spencer was active in the film industry since 1996. As a Black actress, author, and producer, Spencer spent years in front of and behind the big screen, taking on small movie roles and assignments. It wasn't until 2011, when Spencer stared in a movie debut, The Help, she began to receive accolades for her ability as an actress, including an Academy Award, a Golden Globe Award, and three Screen Actors Guild Awards.

For most of us, change seems impossible. But, it is important for us to understand we each have the ability to change at our own discretion. But, let's not forget, there are certain conditions affecting us that are often beyond our control.

Cyntoia Denise Brown, age fourteen, was convicted of killing a man who solicited her for sex. She was sentenced to life in prison. Cyntoia, who served fifteen years in prison, was granted clemency in 2018. She could have chosen to be a victim of her circumstances. Certainly, her circumstances were beyond her control. Instead, Cyntoia overcame her adversity to include redemption, rehabilitation, salvation, mercy, and freedom. She later used her experiences to help other women and girls suffering from abuse and exploitation. Thus, it's often how we endure that shapes the color of our souls.

An Affinity of Spirituality

The color of our souls is reflective of people's intentions, good or bad. For example, any attributions that arise under adverse circumstances reflect our moral character or soul. These attributes give us interest or immediacy. When we notice something interesting about someone, it's often their demeanor, especially as it reflects moral character. Their demeanor has a set of qualities that make them distinctive. When we notice something immediate about someone, we say it's their way; it's their nature. Their disposition or temperament reflects who they are as a person.

When we base attributions on our own experiences or by intuition, what some people describes as a gut feeling, it is the body's way of responding to someone's intentions. In this way, the color of our souls is a metaphor for a set of attributes that reflect the deepest instinctively felt responses (e.g., consciousness, thought, feeling, and will), regarded as distinct from logic or reasoning, or instinctive responses distinct from the physical body.

The color of our souls is an idiomatic phrase characteristic of spoken or written language. We use it to enhance the effect of conversation. When people seem to be wise beyond their years, we call them old souls. It's another way of saying the rebirth of a soul or the cyclic return of a soul destined to live out another life in a new body. Their attributions reflect their moral character.

The color of our souls determines who we are as a whole. In the movie Avatar, the phrase "I see you" was constantly used by the Na'vi as a greeting. Well, it is an old African expression, a form of acknowledgement that means I understand your intentions. In fact, your intentions are a reflection of your soul. Hence, I see you!

Dr. Martin Luther King, Jr. once said, "I have a dream that my four little children will one day live in a nation where they will not be judged by the color of their skin but by the content of their character." In other words, Dr. King was saying, do not criticize my children just because they're Black. Admire them for who they are as a whole. Dr. King wanted White people to understand all children for their attributes. In this way, Whites could learn to appreciate them. Their attributions reflected who they were as a whole. King's speech became a classic in literature because it had a heartwarming message that moved the Civil Rights movement forward. The speech, "I have a dream" also reflected his moral character. Hence, moral character reflects the color of our souls.

What Can We Do To Resolve It?

What we can do to resolve the inhumane treatment of Black people is threefold. First, we need to show a little compassion. A little compassion never hurts anyone. To show kindness or compassion for others reflect the qualities considered to be characteristic of humans as a whole.

People need to consider how much Black people actually suffer. Having the ability to understand their suffering is what enables us show compassion. And, it is our compassion that builds our humanity. The problem with that is many people cannot feel it. That is to say, some people don't have an emotional connection to Black people. They can think through it, logically. They may even be able to reason their way into a strategy for helping them. But many of them lost their ability to feel compassion for the very people they've condemned. So, there goes the display of sympathy needed to feel their suffering, often including the desire to help. For those who fall into this category, there is nothing to wrestle with, no problem to overcome. It is a complete lack of indifference to them whether Black people receive help or not.

It is the lack of dissonance that hold back our humanity, why there is such a struggle to reach the level of humanity necessary to achieve equality for everyone. Unfortunately, they (and by "they" I mean dominant society) believe that today's Blacks are characterized by opposition or antagonism. That many of them are acting out their aggression though open protest and marching demonstrations. The inherited belief is if Blacks were not made submissive by constant harsh treatment, they would dominate White society. They offer the younger generation of Blacks as proof of their natural aggression. Further, they believe oppression fills Black people with hope and humanity.

To the contrary, it's not the duration of hardship or type of suffering experienced that shape and mold Black folk into a courageous and dignified people. Rather, their compassion, courage, and commitment shown in the face of overwhelming adversity create complex human attributes that reflect the color of their souls very clearly. Yet, those who refuse to understand or never had to endure have taken a violent stance against a people for no other reason than to maintain White supremacy, many of them, lacking compassion and causing excessive suffering.

Second, we can also enact laws that ensure the humane treatment of each and every person regardless of race, color, or creed. Humanity is a constant given the evolution of humans. The problem is we, as a species, have yet to fully evolve.

Over the course of millennia, modern humans admixed with Neanderthals, Denisovans, and those belonging to that group. Admixing slowed down the process of human evolution. So, we do not own a monopoly on humanity as of yet. In that way, humanity might just pass us by. The level of kindness or compassion that goes into caring about people is as rare as common sense; and, we do not own the exclusive rights to that, either. In fact, the only people who are fully evolved, that is to say, who are true Homo sapiens (Homo sapien, sapien) are Africans. And, it is our lack of humanity that allows for their suffering.

Problem number three is that the oligarchy believes they are the rule of law. It becomes problematic when the decision-making is made by a select few. The system discourages Commonwealth participation in political decision-making by making distinctions between the popular vote and electoral votes.

What electoral votes do is restrict the exercise of voting by subordinating it to a body of electors. As for the popular vote, well, that simply tells us how many people liked or voted for a particular presidential candidate. In fact, if an overwhelming amount of supporters were to vote for a Presidential candidate or opt to reelect the current President, it doesn't really matter. The Electoral College would have the final say on the matter. Thus, it should be abolished.

Black people are connected to an affinity of the mind, spirit, or soul. Though there are as many layers to it as there are people, their moral character readily reflects who they are as a whole. In my endeavors, I hope to discover the souls of White folk. Why? How we perceive them shapes the color of our souls.

In the introduction, we examined the nature of man and his unrelenting desires to oppress others. In the next chapter, you will learn about the events or life experiences that impact our perceptions, often lasting generations in what we refer to as multigenerational trauma.

Chapter 1
How Multigenerational Experiences Impact Our Lives

In 1863, the Emancipation Proclamation freed slaves held by the Confederacy. After the Civil War, orders were issued to emancipate every slave held across the US nation as implemented under the Thirteenth Amendment. Now, freed Southern Blacks would be subjected to the same conditions as free Blacks in North America—forced to endure the hostility of poor Whites, many of whom did not take likely to the threat of competing with Black people. One freedman, Houston Hartsfield Holloway, wrote about the difficulties of living life in a hostile environment. Hostility was incited by Whites who rejected the notion of living among freed Blacks.

Even with the full cooperation of free Blacks, many of whom participated in the Civil War and still, after the Emancipation Proclamation and two more years of war, Americans could not adjust to the notion of their government accommodating Black people by granting them full US citizenship. Even after Congress called for reconstruction across Southern states (1866 - 1877), implementing plans that would enable Whites and Blacks to coexist as US citizens in a nonslave society, Southern Whites did not welcome new changes and thus resisted. In fact, they resisted to the extent that many Blacks were massacred.

McGuire (in press)

After reconstruction, Black people began to adjust to their circumstances out of necessity. They did not blame God for their circumstances or think prayer would better resolve it. They understood that Black people had some control over their lives. Their duties as newly freed slaves, now US citizens, were to live life to the fullest. Many of them lived fulfilling lives after building their own communities.

It is, again, time for us to reinvent ourselves. Our future rests within younger generations. Now that we're forced to acknowledge the many problems that continue to exist in twenty-first century America, once again, it's time to reflect on how multigenerational experiences impact our lives. We are rethinking an old adage, "Necessity is the mother of inventions," that appears in the dialogue Republic by the ancient Greek philosopher Plato. What Plato meant was we have a need to resolve genuine problems, which encourages creative efforts to meet our present circumstances: our problems. In fact, life experiences help us shape our moral character. Life experiences have a profound or critical influence over our sense of right and wrong and how individual people should behave.

Many experiences, good or bad, past and present, can impact our lives. Each experience has strong, long-term effects on how we coexist in the real world. In other stances, cataclysmic events like war, epidemics, natural disasters, or the death of a loved one have devastating effects that can impact our lives. The results of these events can last generations. That's right; multigenerational experiences can shape the characteristic spirit of future generations.

We can also note the powerful or traumatic social impact of state-sponsored violence. It changed the thinking strategies of many people, especially people of the younger generation to include Blacks but not excluding Whites, Jews, Asians, Arabs or Middle Easterners, LGBTQIAs, even members of the academic community, each group from separate and distinct cultural systems with roots that are impacted by their surroundings. Good or bad, past and present, life experiences have a profound impact on who we are as a whole.

Life experiences shape our fundamental beliefs into a complex system of principled or unprincipled decisions. The ability to make decisions or judgments is essential in determining the fundamental nature of our souls. Fact of the matter is all experiences give us exposure that helps to shape the color of our souls and, often, without awareness of it. Thus, without proper influence, people often find themselves in undesirable situations. The prison industrial complex works as an example.

The Prison Industrial Complex

Since the 1930's, many Blacks were raised in single family households. Most incomes in single families are subsidized. The result is children are often raised in poverty. During which time, they are forced to endure chronic life conditions. The absence of male figures in these families often increases poverty, crime, prostitution, drug abuse, and dropout rates in grade schools. Poor opportunities further disadvantage these children as they become adults to include poor housing opportunities, lack of employment, alcoholism, homelessness, and public handouts just to name a few potent stressors in their lives. The lack of available resources also works to disadvantage generations of poor Black men. And thanks to the Clintons, who built the prison industrial complex, there are more than two million Black men, increasing women, residing in America's prison system.

America's prison systems were expanded to accommodate the high rate of recidivism. Today, the prison industrial complex houses more Black people than were enslaved at the height of US slavery. Now, you can draw two conclusions from the aforementioned. One might first conclude Black people are criminal-minded. We do understand from pseudoscience some people feel Blacks lack the main psychological protective mechanisms necessary to adapt in novel situations. In fact, they believe that maladaptive behaviors found among Black people are due to their inability to adapt after Western civilization tried to civilize them nearly a millennium ago. The other line of reasoning begins with the understanding that Black people are victims of their circumstances.

These people, mainly liberals, believe environment dictates the situation. Given the oppression of slavery and its residual impact on the Black experience, one might further conclude that multigenerational trauma took its toll on the mind-set of Black folk. Yet, Blacks continue to draw strength from the church, value family as a strong source of emotional support, and pride themselves on being sociable and community oriented people. But prison confinement was not the biggest or latest fear among Black folk.

We do know among the greatest fears of Black people is police abuse. Their fears are not out of concern for themselves but their children, many of whom live or came of age while living in single family households. The stress of coping with the potential loss of a loved one has a tremendous impact on them. The daily pounding of being constantly reminded about their situation is also traumatizing to them. Inadequate housing, dangerous neighborhoods, burdensome responsibilities, and economic uncertainties highlight the impact of poverty.

Breonna Taylor, Korryn Gaines, Atatiana Jefferson, and a host of other young Black women were either murdered by law enforcement or died while in police custody. These tragedies give just a glimpse into the pathology of American racism. And I'm not going to bother mentioning the names of young Black males who were murdered by law enforcement or died while in police custody. Their tragic story is reflected in a tireless, endless list of names that should bring shame not only to dominant society but people of the world, many of who continue to stand by and do nothing.

The senseless killing of innocent Black lives awakened many of us. For others, the awakening was so intense that people could no longer cope with it. For example, the constant bombardment of television news on police abuse overloaded their adaptability. Many people simply shutdown because they felt overwhelmed after realizing they didn't know as much as first thought about what fellow citizens endured. Nevertheless, our children will never die in vain. Their voices will be forever echoed in the call for justice. Their memories shape the color of our souls.

Immigrant Rights Violations

The United States is home to the largest immigrant population in the world. Although immigrants assimilate faster in the United States compared to developing nations, lawmakers frequently engage in and appear to enjoy arguments or disputes over immigration policy. Thus, immigration has once again become a highly contentious issue in America. And as America begins to repeat its past, we become fraught with the same problems, dangers, or difficulties.

First term President Donald Trump wanted to build a border-wall. This wall would deter immigrants from entering into the country, illegally. When news of his statement aired on televisions around the world, it started a panic among Hispanic citizens of Central and South America. Many of them packed up their personal possessions and headed to North America in very large numbers.

Most arrived at the US Mexican border by freight train. Others walked for months, hoping to gain entry into the US. Most were stopped at the border. Those who made it into the country illegally were housed at detention centers. Few immigrants, and I mean very few Hispanics, were allowed to live with relatives who were US citizens.

Many more, those who did not meet the criteria of a native Hispanic, were shipped off to other countries, never again to be seen. It was the acceptance of standard criteria used in making the decision or judgment about who would gain entry into the United States I found to be most alarming.

The criteria Hispanics had to meet just to gain entry into the country offended me. The criteria were not made public. But, the only people being turned away or taken away at the border were dark-skinned or Afro-Hispanics. Basically, if they did not have straight hair and or their skin was darker than a brown paper bag, the government escorted them to an airbase, and then put them on the first available flight out of the country, never to be seen or, in most cases, heard from again. Hence, I hasten to imagine, they became some other country's burden.

Now, there were people who lacked compassion for the Hispanic immigrant detainees. Most of them knew many were being taken away to other countries, allegedly. Some knew about Afro-Hispanics being turned away at the US Mexican border, as well. But the lack of compassion shown by Blacks against Hispanics was due to Hispanic Americans and their decision to vote Donald Trump into the Oval Office.

Donald Trump made his position about Black people very clear early on in his presidential campaign. Many Hispanic Americans supported his position. Their decision to support Trump helped him win important votes in the battleground states. Ultimately, Trump won the US Presidential election to become the forty-fifth President of the United States. But, the Hispanic population would soon change their thinking strategies.

Once Trump took office, he began to neglect the Hispanic population. He also treated the Hispanic border detainees inhumanely. "We too are America" was an assertion strongly inspired not solely by the Civil Rights movement but the Black Lives Matter movement as well. Between both movements, Black people inspired a lot of other groups to form powerful movements across the nation. The immigrant rights demonstrations were among the many inspired movements that took place as a result of its impact.

Now, the irony in all of this turmoil is clear. Once the Trump Administration began mistreating Hispanics, many of them realized they were not a part of the Republican agenda. In fact, Hispanics were being disregarded as much as Black Americans. Yet, most of us can't help but feel compassion for the detainees. Our personal history as Black Americans compels us to feel sympathy for their suffering. And, I found, many of us were upset with ourselves for having the desire to help. Our humanity would not allow Black people to standby, idle, and watch in horror the inhumane and brutal mistreatment of strangers or others even though they initially held malicious intentions toward us.

Our compassion for others show the color of our souls—an infectious feeling with an impact that spread throughout the world. But back in America, Latino Civil Rights movements like the farm workers movement, the immigrant rights movement, and the gay rights movement of which they participated, began. These movements were backed up by powerful political organizations like the Mexican American Legal Defense Fund, patterned after the NAACP's Legal Defense Fund. The women's rights movement was also inspired by the shear momentum of the Civil Rights movement. Certainly, our experiences, past and present, provided a powerful template for political activism.

Whenever we feel empathy or sympathy toward another or others, such experiences demonstrate who we are. Building knowledge by modeling or through social learning, or by way of observation and experience, even tender moments like showing sympathy for strangers, feeding the homeless, tutoring the poor, young and old, or doing a random act of kindness exemplify who we are. It is our attributes that make us interesting or distinctive, especially qualities of the heart and mind. But it's not the sum total of life experiences or past thoughts and feelings that make up who we are as a whole. These attributes simply make us socially appealing or not.

State-Sponsored Violence:
White Police Abuse of Authority

We live in a country where the laws are still separate and unequal. But hey, that's okay. Since the early days of the Civil Rights movement to protesting new Jim Crow laws in the new millennium, Black folk made important progress in the name of justice.

The younger generation adapt with such audacity and conviction you immediately come to understand they were born in the face of overwhelming oppression. Since the mounting deaths of Black lives, they took to the streets once again to openly protest police violence, including the senseless killing of George Floyd.

And what a tragedy it was for people to have to protest amid of a pandemic. Unfortunately, the Trump administration reinforced its position on Blacks by sanctioning state-sponsored violence. Since then, police aggressed violently toward anyone who protested in support of Black lives. The increase in hate crime activity and blatant acts of White supremacy were greatly attributable to state-sponsored violence or White police abuse of authority. Many people, not just protesters, believed that police violence and White supremacy laid at the crux of America's terrible oppression. And with police brutality backed by the Trump administration which—at the time, was the highest institution in the land—it seemed more lives would have to be lost before America would resolve this perpetually thorny problem.

Blacks are a resilient people. Even under a new system of oppression—when countless young Black men (increasingly women) were subjected to prolonged abuse and maltreatment at the hands of law enforcement—they were able to recover quickly. They engaged in nonviolent peaceful demonstrations to counter state-sponsored violence, most of which was committed by White police who liked to abuse their authority. Indeed, the younger generation handles oppression with grace and dignity.

Given the near cataclysmic impact police brutality had on Black lives, it would seem America—which has been devastated by the deaths and injuries of countless Blacks—many of them unarmed, were in dire need of change. In order to achieve change or true justice, one of the first steps is to hold police accountable. We need to ensure that law enforcement is held accountable for violence and misconduct.

We do know the system is not broken. Contrary to popular belief, it was designed to do just what it is doing: protect and serve the few privileged Whites it was meant to protect and serve. In other words, the system works for any Westerners having inheritance to everything (W.H.I.T.E. people).

So they fought for George Floyd, Tanisha Anderson, and Philando Castile. They fought for them in the hopes that one day equal protection under the law would not mean Jews need to stay in their own communities or that Puerto Ricans are foreign niggers, or its open season on Black folk. In other words, they hoped change would mandate police officers to protect and serve Black, Brown, and poor people likewise.

We must bring an end to police abuse and state-sponsored violence before we head into another political movement or revolution. Until that day, excessive force by police serves as a constant reminder more work needs to be done, given its significant impact on Black lives.

Coming Out: Gay Lifestyles
And the Rise of Homophobia

Homosexuality has been around since the dawn of time. It is so old, it's older than the world's oldest profession. Few people condemned it throughout history. Yet, people continue to have problems accepting it. So then, why is homosexuality so controversial? What makes gay lifestyles taboo?

In the 1990's, I noticed subtle changes in the perception of young Black folk. Specifically, as dark-skin grew in popularity, young Black people began to love themselves. But, it all started when Sir-Mix-A-Lot produced his debut hit single, Baby Got Back. His rap song changed the dynamics of Black culture. His lyrics were so inspiring, it literately raised the self-esteem of young Black women in America. Many had esteem issues surrounding their body shapes. Coupled with the fact that it was taboo in America to date dark-skinned women, a lot of uplifting and life-affirming experiences had to go into rebuilding the low self-concept and esteem of Black women. When Sir-Mix-A-Lot spoke affectionately about them and their full figured bodies, it suddenly became popular to date dark-skinned women and to prefer Black women with curvaceous bodies. As a result, many Black women began to explore the outer limits of their sexuality.

I thought to myself, how dangerous times were. Self love created envy among my people, one of the capital vices or seven deadly sins. I began to understand how envy could change the perception of people, a vice that already existed among Blacks, but one directed at light-skinned and White people. As Black people loosened their inhibitions, I noticed a steady rise in homosexual activity, largely among Black women. Whatever the reasoning, sometime thereafter, the gay rights movement began.

But how can someone declare, definitively, that this new Black identity was true of women in the younger generation? With Blacks being obligated to the church, honoring the tradition of family, and trying not to rock the proverbial boat, how life-affirming could their experiences be? I mean, really?

Homosexuality on the Rise

The Black community is, perhaps, the most conservative in the United States. Minus the Islamic community, where religion is top priority, Black people value traditional ideas and behavior, perhaps, more so than their conservative White counterparts.

Well, who wants to be subverted, silenced, or pushed back! One of the most courageous things I've seen Black people do is come out of the closet. There is a definite stigma surrounding the adoption of gay lifestyles, especially queer. Queer folk aren't supported in many spaces. But, that doesn't mean they are in anyway less adaptive than anyone else. In fact, queer lifestyle is so fluid it's likely to change at any given moment. And the amount of self-assurance needed to be Black and a femme-identifying lesbian is unbelievable. Many femme lifestyles are unusual yet deserving of attention due to their extraordinary abilities as women. We need to create intentional space for Black femme-identifying and queer-creative folk through uplifting and life-affirming experiences.

People in the Black community have been coming out since the 1990's. Gay rights coalition groups began publicly protesting. They gained so much momentum, a push to openly express their true identity seemed inevitable.

Today, it appears many Blacks have gotten over their homophobic views. Many of the Black churches no longer view gay lifestyles as an abomination. And the gay community seems to be enjoying the fruits of their labor. So then, what's the problem?

Around 2014 to 2017, the Trump era ushered in hate crime activities. In fact, hate crimes based on sexual orientation rose, steadily, to 1,130 incidents over a three year period. Lesbian, gay, bisexual, transgender, queer intersexual, and asexual (LGBTQIA) folk across the country began to experience random acts of violence. Hate crime activity began shifting toward hatred against transgender and nonbinary people. According to the hate crime incidents reported, a large majority targeted were gay men. As late as 2019, at least eleven Black transgender people were killed in nonviolent hate crimes.

The Rise of Homophobia

Trump supporters were also coming out but to express discontent for the LGBTQIA community.

Unfortunately, their bigoted actions started a series of violent antigay hate crimes. Perhaps, Trump's Slogan Make America Great Again (MAGA) helped to fuel the rash of hate crimes. Or maybe his inflammatory use of rhetoric helped to excite contempt among his supporters. Or, was it his election to the US presidency that validated Trump's rhetoric and fueled the idea of hatred among them.

But wait! There is nothing new about gay bashings or hate crimes. Hate crimes are as old as the people who inhabited earth. So then, why do people continue to hate gays even after evolution proves their normative influence on us? Some people developed an irrational hatred or fear of gays and lesbians. Others expressed discontent for gay lifestyles or their culture. Thus, what people were witnessing was the rise of homophobia.

The Trump administration with its right-of-center policies and rhetoric should have been blamed as catalysts for exciting homophobia in America. After Trumps' election, there was an increase in incidents of election-related harassment and intimidation across the country.

Donald Trump even announced on Twitter that he would ban transgender people from serving in the military (2017). He also defended state-funded efforts to ban gay and lesbian couples from adopting children. What does that tell us? It told many people that Trump had homophobic views. And with Trump feeling like he was exempted from punishment, harm, or recrimination, matters were only getting worst.

The style of rhetoric endorsed by the Trump administration was a license to harm folk. Not only was his rhetoric damning to the LGBTQIA community, it was damaging and detrimental to America as a whole. For example, after Trump took office, many of the world's cultures stop conducting business with America. Other countries began to undermine US foreign policy mandates. And, he handled a pandemic poorly. As a result, the US economy was unstable for years.

As for your common, everyday, ordinary homophobes, the LGBTQIA community endured an on-slaught of antigay hate crimes from them. Transgender Black women in Texas endured months of horror. Muhlaysia Booker, a Dallas resident, age twenty-three, was the victim of a hate crime. The assault, recorded on social media, went viral. Weeks later, on the first day of gay Pride or Pride month, Chynal Lindsey, age twenty-six, was found dead. She was the third Black transgender woman murdered in Dallas, Texas, in less than a year.

But in the spirit of pride, many gays, instead of arming themselves or constantly looking over their shoulders, carry on their lives with absolute grace and dignity. Their reality more often means they are the lowest people on the totem pole. So it's chin-up for them, the only way out of their situation is through courage and commitment. Courage and commitment shown in the face of homophobia shapes the color of their souls.

What Can We Do To Resolve It?

One of the things we can do to resolve the problem of our most vulnerable is change their circumstances. We need to consider the impact that multigenerational experiences have on them. Discriminatory practices like racism and homophobia can have a cataclysmic impact that last for generations. The resolution includes, but is not limited to, reducing the amount of discrimination associated with hate crimes.

We would also like to further emphasis that gay lifestyles are inextricably linked to hate crimes. It is important for us to turn our attention to risks that accompany gay lifestyles and to ways that the gay community, especially our queer folk, can cope more effectively with their situation. Their race, culture, and gender identity provides context for the way we need to perceive them. In this way, hate crime laws should be amended soon; so, they can be their authentic selves.

In addition, we need resolve the issue of absentee parents with an emphasis on establishing and improving parent-child relationships in poor families. This resolution has to be a government initiative. First, there should be paternity testing in America to confirm the relationship status of the presumed parents. If both mother and father can confirm the birth status of their presumed child, it will clarify any misconceptions in the future. Paternity testing will also discourage the problem of paternity fraud. In this case, it will reduce court cost.

Further, it will reduce the amount of recidivism so our vulnerable will not relapse into a previous undesirable type of behavior, especially crime. The goal is to change their unfortunate circumstances. The absence of male figures in their lives will only increase the chance they will be affected by their circumstances if the problem is left unresolved. Fewer constraints, better guidance, and more autonomy are the main goals for changing their circumstances.

In the next chapter, we will explore how internalized racism shapes our perceptions. Its impact on finding acceptance is often altered by people's perception of the issue.

Chapter 2
How Internalized Racism Shapes Our Perceptions

The end of the Civil War marked the Period of Reconstruction (1877). During the early period of Reconstruction, a series of violent events occurred in Memphis, Tennessee (1866). It began after a shooting altercation occurred between White policemen and Black Union Army veterans. Mobs of angry White residents and policemen committed a number of riotous acts. They rioted through Black neighborhoods, killing, looting, vandalizing, and committing arson. The 3 day rampage lasted from May 1st to 2nd. The Memphis massacre was the first recorded mass killings of the Reconstruction Period.

Military personnel were called in to bring an end to violence. It took three days to quell the violence so peace could be restored. A follow up report by a joint Congressional Committee concluded that the loss of life included the deaths of 46 Black and 2 white people. Seventy-five Blacks were injured with over 100 Black people robbed, 5 Black women raped, 91 homes, 4 churches, and 8 schools burned down in the Black community. Contemporary estimates place property losses at over $100,000, suffered predominately by Black people. Many Blacks fled the city, permanently. By 1870, their population declined by 1 quarter compared to 1865.

Public consideration following the riots strengthened the argument made by Republicans in Congress. Coupled with recent reports of a massacre committed in July of 1866 in New Orleans, Congress felt stronger action was needed to protect freedmen in the Southern States. The atrocities influenced the passage of the Fourteenth Amendment to the United States Constitution, which granted

Black Americans full US citizenship and equal protection under the law.

The Memphis massacre occurred due to the competition over employment and work-related resources. An investigation into the riots purported that Whites wanted Blacks to return to the plantations to support cotton cultivation with physical labor.

McGuire (in press)

Black people are greatly impacted by American racism. Since the Period of Reconstruction (1866 – 1877), Blacks were left with the difficulties of combating its devastating effects. Many measures were undertaken. Even when confronted with racial conflict and hostility, Blacks showed remarkable resilience and adaptation by developing their own communities and social structures to include Black churches, resource centers, educational institutions, business companies, as well as political, professional, and community organizations. In addition, they learned to conduct effective business with dominant White society. Essentially, they became highly skilled at and developed impressive strategies for adapting to life under the threat or dangers of American racism. Unfortunately, racism continues to evoke anger, grief, and despair for many Blacks today.

Racism is the despair of many Blacks. It often produces profound feelings of hopelessness for them. The problem is America continues to show hostility toward Black people. And mass media has altered the public's perception of the problem. As a result, they experience a feeling or spirit of hostility and resentment from various identity groups.

For example, the brutal killing of Black people by law enforcement reached its height in 2019 just as the corona virus disease 2019 (COVID-19) pandemic affected the lives of everyone. The thought of catching a disease is stressful enough for people. But, as countless Whites began dying from it, news media placed blame on Blacks for supposedly practicing poor hygiene, their reason for its continuation. Thus accusations—compounded with fear and anxiety about the threat and danger of police violence—overwhelmed many. The results were more prejudice, discrimination, bigotry, and animosity directed, primarily, at Black people. Loss of confidence is what caused many to search for social acceptance.

A Struggle to Find
Social Acceptance

Blacks often struggle to find social acceptance. Finding acceptance can be one of the most satisfying feelings imaginable. For example, finding your place in politics can be a rewarding experience. It can be the foundation or basis for further advancement or professional development. Moreover, your affiliation can give a political party a firm footing, which can provide you personal satisfaction or great pleasure. Social acceptance can also lead to an increase in self-efficacy and self-esteem. For example, joining the ranks of law enforcement can give someone a feeling of kinship and closeness. Closeness often teaches a person to have compassion for strangers and others.

For the most part, social acceptance is a normal, healthy human experience. In fact, the emotional state of acceptance is an acknowledgment that in some way a life is renewed and filled with a new sense of purpose. For example, the organization Black Lives Matter renewed their campaign to revamp America's police force. The campaign was motivational to many people who were looking to achieve a higher level of comfort or stability. The down side of finding social acceptance is the tendency to dismiss as unimportant other people's worth or self-concept.

Blacks who feel they get along with Whites much better than members of their own race are preoccupied with finding social acceptance. Unfortunately, it is a long-standing practice of Whites to exclude Black people from social acceptance unless they are part of the cultural mainstream. However, there are a few exceptions. Take Candace Owens, for example.

Candace Owens will probably be accepted into mainstream culture. Candace Amber Owens Farmer is a conservative American, an author, commentator, and political activist. She was initially critical of President Donald Trump and the Republican Party. But, she became known for speaking out in support of dominant White society. As an African American woman, her sensibilities were frazzled due to the continued killing of Blacks by law enforcement. Curiously, she blamed Black people for being brutally mistreated. She accused them of being criminal-minded. Her resolution was to limit the amount of interaction between them and law enforcement.

Candace proposed to reduce the amount of criminal activity Black people engaged in. She believed there would be no cause to stop and detain Black people on the grounds of suspicion if they reduce the intent of criminal activity. The problem with her theory is that the stop-and-frisk laws allowed any Black person to be stopped and detained on the bases of skin color, be the intent of activity suspicious or not. Candace—who views herself as a modeled minority—also made countless accusations about the crisis in Black leadership.

Social acceptance draws on the many intricacies society gains from the exploitation of others. Acceptance is a crucial indicator of assimilation. Since 1954, for instance, Democrats have taken on the responsibility of integrating Blacks into mainstream culture. However, Republicans have long since argued America has taken on a social liability by accepting people who are perceived to function beneath the norm, especially on valued dimensions. Unfortunately, our natural tendency to accept ideas, customs, practices, or people as potentially beneficial or problematic is realistically influenced by our personal experiences. Therefore, we have a need to believe people and their experiences should be morally correct (truthful) or valid (useful) in nature before we can accept them.

Understanding Internalized Racism

Unfortunately, Candace Owens was not of the culture. Nor was she for the people. She was impacted by negative experiences in the Black community. Her anger and resentment was directed at the very people said to have abandoned her. Her bitter retort was said in quick response to accusations of her loyalty to political conservatism and the Republican Party. She's been called a mammy archetype due to her unwavering commitment. The symbolic transfer of negative emotions from White to Black was how she displaced unwanted aggression.

In theory, an unjustified negative attitude toward members of one's own race more likely stems from being rejected by them. In this way, the individual will come to treat his or her own people unfairly. If his or her position is harbored for an extended period of time, it is enough for the individual to develop self-defeating thoughts. The individual would then struggle to overcome his or her feelings of inferiority. He or she would then need to displace his or her aggression onto members of his or her race. Displaced aggression is needed to remove any dissonance from his or her way of thinking. In the case of Candace, she displaced her socially inadequate feelings onto other Blacks who became implied or imagined problem sources.

The psychology of victimization endured by Candace—even before choosing to endorse the Republican Party—led to her inability to adequately deal with Black people and more than we might expect. I refer to this state of victimization in my book, The Ignoble Paradox of Man, as internalized racism:

> *Internalized racism* is a psychopathological state that develops [from] exposure to traumatic events (like slavery or apartheid), severely oppressive situations (like in the case of poverty or prison incarceration), severe abuse (as in rape or police brutality), natural disasters (Hurricane Katrina, for example), or accidental disasters (like the Rockefeller coal-mining catastrophe in West Virginia, per se).

Internalized racism is described by feelings of *self-hatred*: an emotional disturbance resulting from one's own efforts. Here, people make negative attitudes or behavior part of their existence. Internalized hatred is then learned or assimilated through unconscious bigotry. Social anxiety disorders like self-defeating thoughts, self-fulfilling prophecy, self-abuse, and self-betrayal—for which dependent males can manifest though aggression in an exaggerated effort to retain self-control—are symptoms of a disturbance that immediately follows the trauma. At other times, the onset of trauma can be delayed by months, years even. A particular feature of this trauma is largely identified and described by a suffering inflicted from self-hatred.

We now recognize any sociocultural influences that internalize negative feelings—fragment the psyche and its functions—as dimensions of self-hatred. We demonstrate the presence of racism by how well people of color are accepted in society.

Identity Problems that
Come From Having A
Low Self-Concept

The color line has always been an exclusive problem of Black Americans; but today, it's becoming a concern to many. Black people represent a widely growing, ever diversifying segment of American society. The idea that they will not reach or live up to their potential, are destined to make fewer contributions in ways society doesn't need, and refuse to take their place as productive citizens, was created under the fear that Black people, if allowed to rebuild their economic resources and own communities, will diminish the power of White Americans. Thus, White people want Black people to be teased apart from mainstream culture rather than have them live in concert.

Even today, in twenty-first century Western civilization, two Americas continue to exist: one inherently White and the other unapologetically Black. The rise of the Ku Klux Klan and lynching, Aryan gangs and church burnings, protest from both sides, the Civil Rights movement, the Black Panther Party and their movement, and a few Black liberation struggles in between proved no side showed any regret or sorrow for their counterpart's past sins, aggressions, or unfortunate circumstances. But, I remember a time when, somewhere amid finding our identity and developing a low self-concept, Black people were penitent about their existence and hated their own people.

People fail to understand the magnitude of problems associated with self-hatred. Have you ever wondered why some people refuse to identify with their own race? There is a terrible social stigma surrounding race in America. And, many people of color, those of whom can pass for some other race, often do.

Passing is a way for Black people to escape social exclusion and persecution by dominant White society. As a dimension of cultural assimilation, it is a process in which a racial group, its members, or an individual person takes on the cultural traits of the dominant society. Except in this case, passing more often comes from a person who wants no further conflict in his or her life.

Many people who pass for White often learn to discriminate against members of their own race. They often do as a way of warding off Whites who may be suspicious of their racial identity. People who pass are especially resistant to anyone who may upset the status quo. That people feel they have to cloak their identity in racial secrecy is a sad reality we must bear. To talk about the ill-effects of low esteem that comes from discriminating against your own people is dangerous in and of itself.

But to seek out acceptance from a society that may be unnecessary for the preservation or emergence of a new identity is problematic. In this way, the need to isolate one's self from friends and family—just because his or her racial identity is a perceived violation of cultural expectations—requires further consideration. Unfortunately, people of color will continue to pass until they achieve true equality on the world stage.

Historically, Black people struggled with identity problems. Low self-concept and esteem started when they lost their identity during the enslavement process.

Colorism: A Dimension of Self-Hatred

Colorism was a heuristic function widely regarded by slave masters in the United States. In this case, light skinned slaves (house niggers) who were usually the offspring of a slave master would be allowed to benefit from less strenuous domesticated duties. In contrast, the darker, grimmer slave (field niggers) endured hard, manual labor.

After abolitionists emancipated Blacks from slavery, Blacks developed methods of weeding out dark skinned people from light skinned people who were thought to have a chance of passing for White. They would conduct a comparative analysis by holding up a brown paper bag next to the face of a Black person to see if the skin tone was light enough to be accepted by Whites. This antiblack ritual was common practice during the early 1900's among affluent Black Americans and their families.

Howard University, in Washington, DC, a prestigious historically Black educational institution, practiced colorism. As evidence, Howard University once required Black applicants to submit a photograph of themselves in order to ensure new students met the social standards to achieve among Whites and other European Americans. Spike Lee's innovative, yet offbeat, music-filled, contemporary 1988 Broadway style comedy, "School Daze," accurately depicted self-conflict struggles between lighter and darker skinned students on historically Black college and university campuses. As depicted in School Daze, neither sororities nor fraternities would allow those whose skin color was darker than a brown paper bag admission into college societies.

The Brown Paper Bag Test also has guidelines for social acceptance among the lighter Blacks, which includes the "comb test," a procedure that establishes the person's hair coarseness, and the "flashlight test," which examines a person's facial profile to ensure his or her features were comparable to Whites. Internalized hatred socializes the perception of standards among Blacks at colleges and universities across America.

My first encounter with colorism occurred in the fifth grade. A girl who wanted to be my friend was offset by her grandmother. Her grandmother told her she could only be my friend if I passed the brown paper bag test. I do not recall how the conservation transpired but in the end, while I was unaware of it, she held a brown paper bag up to my face to make a quick comparison. She quickly tried to claim me down after I passed the test. Needless to say, we never did become friends. I do believe her mother took one look at me and told her my skin would darken in a few years. So, I fell out of favor with her and her family. Hence, that was the first time I understood how colorism or self-hatred affected my people's self-concept.

I was mortified by my first experience with colorism. From that time onward, I've been acutely aware of how our people internalize racism to the point of self-hatred. There would be many times I found myself combating racism against my own people. But, that happened in the early 1980's.

Now, sometime in the 1990's, dark-skin grew in popularity. Black men started noticing the beauty of dark-skin Black women. The courtship would begin with a crude statement like, "Hey, you're cute to be dark," as if it were a rarity to find beauty among dark-skinned women. Black women responded in kind by saying, "He's cute, being light skinned and all," as if to put a premium on light-skin as the norm of beauty. Even today, there are Blacks who will not date dark-skinned people due to self-hatred. Some even say they will not have children unless their mate is extremely light or White. The fear is having children who are as dark as them. And who can say, never having lived in their skin, anything about how internalized racism shapes their perception.

Black people have been dealing with identity problems since the end of US chattel slavery. Niggers, Negros, colored people, Black American, African American with and without the hyphen, and for those who experienced cognitive dissonance, people of color. I, personally, prefer Black American as a racial identity as many Africans I've encountered chose not to identify with native Black folk in America. Just ask the average African, "What's an Acata?" You can Google it! An Acata is a Black person who is said to have convened with jackals.

And, any good Christian can tell you the symbolism of jackals.

The Notion of Colorblindness

"I don't even notice that you're Black!" I don't see color! People are all the same to me! The problem with these statements is each one is untrue. When people make statements like the aforementioned, it is symptomatic of a greater problem. You never hear White people tell Asians, I don't notice you're Asian. And, you'll never hear Black people tell a White person, I never even notice you're White. In fact, people only make these statements when they're uncomfortable with someone's racial identity. Hence, the untrue statement, "I'm colorblind!" What we need to do in order to understand people's psychology is look at the pathology surrounding the issue of race.

Dr. Joy DeGruy had an interesting philosophy that read:

> Truthfulness is the foundation of all human virtue. American pathology is our denial. It is what keeps us sick around the issue of race. …If you cannot tell me the truth, then we cannot trust each other; and, if we cannot trust each other, then we cannot have a relationship; and, if we don't have a relationship, we have nothing.

So, when people say they don't see color or they're colorblind, in fact, they're speaking an untruth. They have an intrinsic feeling of discomfort, uneasiness, and fear surrounding the issue of race. The general concern is they view skin color as problematic when assigning blame to people of color. Thus, that statement is an admission that their own behavior, when interacting with people of color, is displeasing and needs to be resolved to a consonance. So, use of colorful terms is another way for Whites to maintain control of the narrative. The point is White people don't help when they create catchphrases that further denigrate the Black identity.

Whites have a continued need to give their accounts of unjustifiable abuse and trauma committed by their people. Their explanations help them to reduce the lack of consistency or compatibility between their actions and their beliefs. In this way, the term obscures criticism of violence, inequality, and injustice readily found in America's social system.

Colorblindness is supposed to be a public avowal not to view skin color as a deficit. It is suppose to be an oath to condemn historical racism. People following this school of thought are said to reject discrimination with the intention to discredit racism, prejudice, bigotry, and homophobia.

But upon further inspection, use of the term colorblindness is evident that White people have an extrinsic problem coping or interacting with people of color. To not notice or acknowledge someone's skin color, one would literately have to be blind or unable to recognize and adequately deal with extrinsic reality.

For example, when White people changed Black Lives Matter to All Lives Matter, it represented a statement denying any or all accusations of wrongdoing, that all lives were victims of racial abuse and inequality. Yet, all lives were not. The assumption behind victimization or victimhood demeaned and trivialized suffering among Blacks as understood to be too accepting or readily willing. The increase of official murders, resulting from thoughtless, impetuous behavior, exposed the truth behind colorblindness. Confronted with this blinding clarity of knowledge, a resolution seems nearly impossible.

What Can We Do To Resolve It?

What can we do to resolve the problem of racism when it's motivated by self-hatred? What happens when we internalize the beliefs and values of the very people who impose it? How do we resolve the problem of internalized racism, especially when it shapes our perceptions?

First, it's the way we consider racism that makes it complicated and difficult to resolve. We have a tendency to see negativity or the worst aspects of life and expect to endure certain levels of unpleasantness. But to find a resolution to racism, we need to understand that it provides the basis or outline for a system of oppression by which America is built. In this way, racism will not end anytime soon.

However, we can inhibit it from being expressed. But, we must attach some of the responsibility to dominant society. By attaching some of the responsibility to the very people who benefits from it, we hold them accountable. In this way, we even hold those accountable who are not generally aware of it but may manifest themselves by engaging in dissociated acts. We do not need to find a new medium that can decipher codified languages just to better understand how racism is used to impact Black people and their psyche. This, we already know! Instead, we can achieve moral culpability by searching within the framework of the Black prophetic tradition.

Second, we must look into the health and wellness of our children. This means we must focus attention on our precious young, many of whom engage in youthful indiscretions, especially because of a cynicism or distrust they have for White people. Many of them also hold grim beliefs about their future in America. The ability of our young to live and grow or to continue in existence depends, largely, on revitalizing cherished traditions, perhaps, even creating a new framework and languages to help them understand the beauty of being Black people. In this way, we need to challenge ourselves.

The utter disregard for Black people comes from holding Christian beliefs or of being a Christian. Christianity argues against the truth or correctness of Black history and the rich prophetic tradition of Black people. Now pardon my French; but, Black history teaches us that Europe never produced a religion nor did its people have the ability to create a prominent religion like Christianity. Black history also teaches us that the name Jesus did not exist in antiquity because the letter "J" was not a part of Jewish language and was used indecisively among Europeans until the late 1400's or early 1500's. And while

Pope Innocence the VIII was responsible for encouraging the enslavement of African people, I do believe it was Pope Alexander, VI, who used his son as a symbol of worship and image of Christ. As the story goes, Pope Alexander was tired of his people praying to a Black savior (Ye'shua). Remember, when the Pope prays, he prays to a Black Madonna. In this way, Christianity is based on a body of Christian doctrines we accept as gospel without written evidence.

Pope Julius II headed the Roman Catholic Church and ruled the Papal States (1503 – 1513). He commissioned Michelangelo to create a Europeanized version of Christ. Had Michelangelo refused, the Pope promised to behead him and have his remains brought to his chambers on a silver platter. Michelangelo, who had no conception of a White Christ, used his homosexual lover as the model for the imagery. He painted a mural of Christ on the ceiling of the Sistine Chapel.

What does a long drawn out paragraph on Christianity has to do with our earlier discussion? When we're taught that God is White, the Virgin Mary is White, and White people are a direct reflection of their existence, it shapes the perception of our young who are being taught they have yet to make any contributions to this world. And such untruth is already being reinforced by Black people from older generations. To adopt the beliefs, values, and attitudes of our oppressors, either consciously or unconsciously, clearly comes from having a disregard for ourselves.

Self-hatred is clearly the cause of blame or failure for the tragic plight of our young Black people, many of whom endure chronic life conditions. For example, our young are ten times more likely to live in poverty than their White counterparts. Most of our young who suffer from poverty as children will endure it for a period of about twenty years. Poverty also forces our young to endure threatening and uncontrollable life events. These events undermine the sources of social support that take part in protecting our young folk from the overwhelming stress of oppression.

Last, we must develop a positive self-perception. We have been taught to show consideration for White people as well as their wellness and personal interests, especially when placed before ourselves and other people. In this way, Blacks develop a sense of duty and honor. We serve our oppressors in their armed forces. We serve their communities as civil servants. We also stand in protest to benefit other identity groups. One thing we never had going for ourselves is a chance to heal, spiritually or emotionally.

Our enduring injuries are the reasons why we struggle to gain acceptance and more than any identity group in American society. Oddly, social acceptance seems to be a simple enough emotion. Yet, I must admit its complexity is not a superficial feeling one has in passing, but a need to be respected, approved, cherished, and esteemed (R.A.C.E.).

One of the most negative outcomes of not being accepted is internalized racism or self-hatred otherwise the adoption beliefs, values, and attitudes of an oppressor, either consciously or unconsciously, especially as perceived by strangers and others. In this way, we have a catastrophic love affair with our oppressors who use our injuries to gain leverage and keep control over Black people. It can manifest in a variety of behaviors like self-hatred, self-defeating thoughts, self-fulfilling prophecy, self-abuse, and self-betrayal. A prime example we use to illustrate its negativity is colorism.

Colorism is a prejudice or discrimination against individuals who have dark skin tone, typically among people of the same race. Within the Black community, colorism is a serious psychopathology that needs to be resolved.

Colorblindness, as the last example of racism, is the antithesis of what is needed to repair or rectify our injuries. It also helps White people to justify their feeling of discomfort, uneasiness, and fear of Black people. It is important for us to turn our attention to problems associated with cognitive dissonance and to the ways that poor Black people might be influenced by it.

Unless we can heal the rift within ourselves, there stands little chance for us to progress as a people. It's also important for us to understand how cognitive dissonance affects various identity groups as a whole.

In the next chapter, we will explore racism and various dimensions of racial violence. Individual, institut-ionalized, and cultural racism are topical discussions in chapter 3. Racial conflict and hostility highlights the remainder of the next chapter.

Chapter 3
Racism and the Various Dimensions of Racial Violence

On March 9, 1892, three of Ida Bell Wells-Barnett's friends were brutally lynched in Memphis, Tennessee. The three men were successful business partners who managed a grocery store, The Peoples' Grocery, just outside of Memphis at a location known as "the curve." A rivaling White grocery store owner by the name of Barrett charged them with conspiracy. News of their accusal spread quickly throughout the Black community as the three men, along with several other Black supporters, were arrested and jailed for making verbal threats against Whites. Quarrelsome battles brewed for several days as the three store owners were rearrested for inciting riots. In their several days of captivity, they were brutally beaten and denied visitation rights. Afterwards, select members from the White community (the lynch mob) broke the trio out of jail, carted them off about a mile, shot them dead, and then hung them by their necks as a semblance of justice. It was said that their last words were turn my head west so that I may face freedom.

The brutal murder of all three men compelled Ida to reevaluate the psychopathology of each lyncher and to realign her own ideology in hopes of ascertaining some truth. At the time, many Americans, both White and Black, believed Black males were hung for accosting and raping White women. Oddly enough, these men had not been accused of rape or accosting White women. In fact, they were pillars of the community, noblemen, whose only crime had been economic prosperity. Ida, distraught by the event, investigated and discovered their murders were an emblematic design devised from ethnic cleansing.

Who would commit such heinous acts of aggression and brutality? When will there ever be a time for peace in this country? Why are some people so indifferent in their beliefs they cannot interact with people outside their own cultural group? How does a nation seek to justify such horrible and savage acts against its own members while at the same time calling its actions fair or just? These questions are important to the survivability of American society. If you ever asked any of the above questions, then you are concerned with racism and the various dimensions of racial violence.

McGuire (in press)

This book has unique cultural dimensions to help us make sense of our increasingly complex and challenging world. It's not that Black folk simply refuse to adapt; we live in a hostile society that is becoming an increasingly harder place in which to live. For instance, the topic of hate crimes never gets old, is multifaceted, and thus forever changing in appearance. And with the continuous abuse and violence directed at Black citizens, the United States can no longer think of itself as a fair or just society. Ironically, as racism becomes more and more overt, so do our concerns for Black lives, and with the growing amount of concerns, we develop stronger kinships that strengthen family and friendship bonds. The downside is our inability to feel compassion for those outside of our supportive network.

Our society is also becoming increasingly diverse. And with greater diversity comes greater concerns for competition. We can help reduce conflict and meet a wide range of challenges simply by trying to find answers to such questions. Throughout this chapter, you will learn how racism and the various dimensions of racial violence impact our lives.

Racism and Racial Violence

Racism continues to present itself as a problem in this rapidly growing and diverse culture. In contemporary forms, racism continues to impact significantly on the lives of Americans. Old-fashion racism, however, is still an upsetting and surprising event or experience.

We now know racism, especially in women, was made to appear less aggressive than it is in actuality. As we continue to learn from the contents of this chapter and throughout our continued discussion, racism is a complete change of direction in how people behave, think, and feel. Still, we will see how persistent people are in reinforcing myths and stereotypes about Black people. Blacks are still typecast as socially incompetent, bitter, and angry to the very end of reasoning despite continuous efforts to inform and educate.

Racism is etched into the minds of many people. Feelings of superiority can be blatant as believing all Blacks are unintelligent and incapable of making informed decisions. Or, it can be a subtle lighting of clever and indirect discrimination by giving them a pat on the back instead of opportunities they deserve. Thus *racism,* as a form of inequality, describes any unjust attitude, behavior, or experience backed by institutional power. Aggression often encourages apathy and maltreatment of Blacks due to race or skin color.

What's more concerning, however, is the unjust thinking that leads to racial violence. In this case, a person may harm, injure, or kill people they may know—school mates, peers, neighbors, colleagues, coworkers, associates, and acquaintances—for instance. James Byrd Jr. was dragged to his death by three White supremacists, all of whom he knew. At other times, racial violence is merely a random act of aggression.

For example, Susan Smith strapped her children into their car-seats. She then pushed her car into a lake, drowning them. Susan, certifiably insane, made up a story, accusing two Black men of kidnapping her children during a carjacking. With the help of a sketch artist, the police found and arrested two suspects living five states away. Police charged both men with multiple crimes to include murder of her two children. It was later discovered that Susan Smith made up the entire story to cover her own fiendish deeds.

The point I'm making here is *racial violence* is based on a system of advantage, backed by institutional power. Susan Smith had the power to adversely impact the lives of two Black men she never knew simply because she was White. James Byrd, Jr. was dragged to his death until his body dismembered. Why? He was Black and therefore vulnerable. From a Black person's perspective, racial violence can be seriously harmful and maladaptive as it is multidimensional.

Between the years 1850 and 1960, five thousand Black Americans were lynched in a wave of violence. Like Mr. Byrd, many of these victims knew their attackers.

Various Dimensions
of Racism

James M. Jones (1971-1995) proposed a three part explanation for racism. Individual, institutionalized, and cultural dimensions supported his life course theory. Consequently, while Jones believed institutionalized racism was the most dangerous, giving birth to all existing degrees, dimensions, successions, and aggressions, individual racism is what gave the mental impression of hate and persecution.

Individual Racism

Individual racism can be described as hatred and persecution toward, hostility for, antagonism against, or an aversion that reflect bad impressions of relationships or communication between a group or certain members due to their racial origin or skin color. Individual racism is an invidious moral reasoning identified by its systematic arrangements of ascribed associative dimensions to include fear or denial, intolerance, separation, segregation, prejudice, discrimination, oppression, and racial hatred.

These dimensions are affects of mass media, culture, and society. For instance, people characterized by individual racism may feel Blacks and Hispanics are inherently lazy and very dishonest. They may also believe Blacks and other minorities lack the intelligence or mental fortitude to function productively in a modernize society. As a result, many are forced to except public handouts. Individual racists are said to organize and participate in public protest, even taking aggressive actions against people of color. All dimensions that recognize attributes, characteristics, abilities, or qualities specific to each race, overlap with individual racism.

Institutionalized Racism

Institutionalized racism is a psychology and product of Western civilization. Discovery of this method was popularized by civil right activist Stokely Carmichael (Kwame Ture) and political scientist Charles Hamilton who coined the term in the 1960s. It is more systemic than individual racism. Formally, *institutionalized racism* can be described as a system of behavior and beliefs that one group can oppress another by way of subjugation and exploitation and by claiming biological differences. It is an expression of hatred that occurs in any institution under such public bodies as families, corporations, or universities.

Institutionalized racism differs from the traditional dimensions in that it deals with systemic policies and practices that disadvantage people of color. Housing agreements and loan policies along with barriers to employment and upward mobility of Black people are examples. Note the emphasis on systematic dimensions. Its structure—the arrangement and relations between parts of governing bodies—is what makes institutionalized racism the most dangerous of conceptual movements, not just the actions of bigotry found in other oppressive dimensions. Other, more historical, examples of institutionalized racism are as follows:

- The Social Security Act of 1935: It was passed to guarantee legal rights to income for retirement workers. Unfortunately, it specifically excluded domestic and agricultural workers, most of whom were African American, Mexicans Americans, and Asian Americans, from retirement incomes. This Congressional Act lessened minorities' opportunities to pass wealth onto the next generation.

- In the 1930s, race was included into the decision to increase property value and loan eligibility of US citizens. This was collaborated by the US property appraisal system. As a result, only the highest of property value ratings were given to historically White communities and White people became eligible for government loans. From 1934-1962, less than a fraction of subsidized housing was distributed to Blacks, poor people, and the vulnerable.

These examples are methods involving social exclusion used to disadvantage people of color from certain entitlements of institutions. There does not have to be any reasonable intention for certain races to benefit or be disadvantaged by institutionalized racism. The intent is intertwined and mutually exclusive with the training and doctrine of many institutional policies.

Cultural Racism

Cultural racism refers to hatred or contempt a society has for the social customs, institutions, accomplishments, and accommodations given to people of color. With cultural racism, customs, institutions, and achievements of minorities are viewed in some way as flawed and impeded by performance and productivity. For instance, Jamaicans are viewed by Whites to be backwards in terms of progress because many continue to practice in pagan religions like voodoo. Also, Black and Latina women are viewed to have children out of wedlock and Whites believe that infidelity hurts development toward better, more complete, modern social conditions.

Further, they are assimilated into the social system of a dominate culture, which suggest they are not well-adjusted enough to fully function in mainstream society. Through *assimilation*, minorities are absorbed into a dominate group, which often means loss of some or all behaviors and values from their original group. In short, loss of behavior, values, and belief systems usually occur as a result of *accommodation* or attempts to adjust to new, cultural-specific types of information.

In sum, the various dimensions of racism, in and of themselves, are processes for understanding intergroup relations. Further, understanding various dimensions help to better ascertain those social arrangements we build around our concrete physiological limitations to prevent an *adverse physiological response* (like fight or flight), a *reaction* (fear or anger, for example), or *defensive gesture* (i.e., cringe or posture).

Or, it can be environmental conditions that form experiences in which our physiological needs are triggered into acts of aggression or violence. The topic of racism will fluctuate with the passing of time as have all other topical discussions in the past. The temporal change in social discourse varies with prevailing trends (cultural patterns in which experiences are developing or changing behavior) and cultural attitude.

The rest of this chapter discusses various dimensions of racial aggression. Hate crimes, racial conflict, and racial hostility often lead to racial violence. All existing degrees, dimensions, successions, and aggressions are dimensions of racism.

The Rise of Hate Crimes

According to Christian doctrine, homosexuality is an abomination before God. Therefore, ministers and Church congregations, at one point, believed gays will burn in hell for all eternity. What's more disturbing is that people now feel Jews contribute to certain problems of inequality. They contend Jews are taking the place of racists in America, and this problem will lead to more racial violence.

For instance, Eliyahu and Avi Werdesheim, Jewish brothers, were arrested for the beating of a young Black teenager. The Werdesheim brothers were patrolling a Jewish community in Park Heights, Baltimore, Maryland as part of a neighborhood watch group when they stopped and openly attacked a Black teen for walking home through their neighborhood. Eliyahu, the oldest at twenty-four, was sentenced to three years probation.

The Rise of Hate Crimes

America didn't understand the concept of hate crimes until about 1980 when emerging supremacy groups like the Skinheads began a wave of violence against Black people.

FBI Crime reports cited evidence of hate crimes as showing an increase in frequency, and incidences reflected current social trends. In fact, there were 7,783 incidents of hate crimes reported for the year 2008. Before you propose whether hate crime statistics suggest America is becoming laden with racial violence—whereby members opposed to the existence of a particular identity group will engage in activities involving physical force intended to hurt, injure, or even kill—two important factors must first be understood: (1) A large majority of racial violence is being committed by White Americans and (2), research suggest the rise in hate crimes is expected to increase with national diversity. In fact, the chance of diversity inciting hate crimes between groups largely depends on how well America learns to cope with devastating events like recessions.

The Rise in Racial Violence

When hate groups experience unfairness, each will develop feelings of intense dislike for women, lesbians, gays, and other identity groups. These feelings are accompanied by a strong need to retaliate in violence against those they, in some way, hold responsible. Moreover, violence appears to be influenced by certain roles and expectations of the cultural in-group, required as appropriate or rightfully due. For instance, unrealistic expectations about conservatism or Western tradition have in the past caused conflict differences between identity groups. When these groups cannot reach a compromise, perceived incompatibility between certain beliefs and opinions of existing members is shown to increase the rate by which violence occurs. In fact, racial conflict appears to beget violence as if change or acceptance bares an unconscionable compromise.

Hidden factors—which appear to play a significant role in racial violence—involve change or the threat of compromise via acceptance in society: integration, same-sex marriage, immigration, minority hiring, and social competition, for instance. In theory, change causes a great amount of violence from a perceived loss of one's identity.

Change also produces negative reactions in children who feel socially compromised (e.g., those with parents who are dealing with job lost, forced to move into a new home environment, coping with divorce or a new stepparent, or bereft of a loved one). It appears possible that the inability to adequately cope with change, displayed through negative reactions, contributes to an increase in violence. Since these experiences may in fact translate into conflict or even hostility, the incidence of racial violence is likely influenced by attrition in cultural development.

This degree of aggressive motivation is ideal because the victimizer tends to single out people of color to either control or exploit them. The reasoning behind this method of violence is intended to coerce or intimidate their victims. Thus, it ensures servility and passivity among identity groups like Blacks while preventing their movement between occupations, places of residents, or improving socioeconomic conditions in the future. In short, racial violence reduces the likelihood victims will compete for social competency against dominant White society.

Why are people of color singled out for unfair treatment? Whether we proposed dominant society or at least certain members are on a power trip, we would not be too far off from discovering an appropriate answer. We do know motives play an important role. That is, people are hostile toward people of color because their motives are to wield power or affirm their in-group status position. We can speculate about certain dimensions of group integrity: the desire to seize power, feelings of membership or belongingness, attitudes toward racial integration, and the tendency to be unhappy or depressed (we do know being in uncontrollable situations often causes depression).

Hostility That Begets Violence

Deliberate hostility for dominant society tends to increase because of differences that exist between identity groups. Personal desires are often involved in gaining some influence over other people and becoming powerful group-wise or to obtain in-group status position. Feelings of depression do not appear to enter into the equation for dominant society. With Blacks and other identity groups, however, it is quite possible all three motives for being hostile are present. For dominant society, aggression against those who are perceived to be lower in status may counter the negative effects of depression.

Depression is believed to internalize as self-defeating thoughts in women and externalize as aggression for men. There are other, more discerning factors in racial hostility. However, motives found here play a major role in many different contexts. But, these motives are thought to be cause-inducing factors for racial hostility in all situations.

Perhaps, a common sense question would point out beyond motives for power and belonging, what other reasons would dominant society have for showing hostility. In the case of hate groups, there is a tendency to be hostile toward minorities because most believe they show maladaptive traits. Conversely, victimized groups tend to believe hate groups, like Aryans, supremacists, and other right-winged extremists, behave the way they do because for some odd reason they're experiencing cultural nihilism.

In this case, principles are dismissed as being unworthy of careful consideration from the cultural in-group because new, socially acceptable attributions appear to be lower than desirable. Here, attributions play an important role in how people react in social situations because they tend to perceive intentions or motives as hostile and threatening, especially when people's actions are thought provoking. In a sense, hate groups will attack women, lesbians, gays, and people of color because they believe people who differ from the majority in race, sex, gender, and so forth are particularly dangerous. As a result, they will engage in violence to protect their in-group status position.

Another explanation for hostility by dominant society is the tendency to project their opposing intentions onto strangers and others lower in ability as a way to protect self-esteem. Dominant society projects onto others by justifying their behavior. Next, they relabel the people who they would like to oppress. Relabeling is done in such a way that justifies their behavior toward the intended group. As a result, dominant society often become manipulative and shows no compassion toward the oppressed. Thus, empathizers who do not trust people of color, feel totally vindicated when hate groups take unfair advantage of them.

Are these motivations common or displaced aggression? *Cultural abuse*—cultural nihilism and a degree of violence in which the victim is treated poorly or cruelly—proposes an obvious explanation. In this case, dominant society will usually speak to Blacks in an insulting and offensive manner. It occurs not only between members of dominant society and those lower in status, but also among low socioeconomic or minimal groups, as well. *Cultural abuse* includes such actions as improper use or exploitation of minorities, social exclusion, cruelty and maltreatment (particularly, in the case of public and private ridicule), invading personal space, rude and discordant behavior, making intentionally false statements, and winning praise or attention for oneself by preempting a minority's attempt to attain credit. In fact, if anyone can identify with any example from the aforementioned, then they too are victims of cultural abuse.

When cultural abuse occurs, it can take place within these three cognitive domains:

- *Antagonism*: Conflict can occur by resistance or dissent, lack of sensitivity, or refraining
from interacting or trying to prevent an argument.

- *Obstructionism*: The victimizer will also show aggression intended to prevent or hinder the victim's wellness (e.g., such aggression can be blatant as cross burnings, abortion bombings, or threatening phone calls, or subtle attitudes like failure to return calls and interfering with America's infrastructure).

- ***Racial hostility***: If one person is hostile toward a victim, the individual will show an unjust attitude that is intended to be evil or harmful (e.g., cultural abuse or insults, destruction or theft of property, a stated intention to inflict injury, damage, or other implied aggression toward the victim like dismissing their opinions as unimportant, discussing victims without their knowledge, et cetera).

These dimensions were regarded with intensity by dominant society but, today, are greatly reduced in frequency through government legislation. Cultural abuse is less likely to result in physical assaults, today, even though the incidence of violence is increasing. In addition, people of color often encounter cultural abuse caused by dominant society.

Cultural abuse occurs in much the same way as racial violence. Since government legislation may be the only viable means of controlling racial violence, understanding cultural abuse becomes especially important. A special note of importance: Cultural abuse, today, is characterized more by exploitation than hostility or violence. But, we'd still like to know some of the cause-arousing factors. We believe sociocultural factors contribute to poor communication during racial conflict, which begets violence.

Some majority individuals and hate groups believe the best way to meet conflict is with racial violence. They believe, in some way, Black people have provoked them. So, racial violence against Black people is perceived to bring these supporters and hate groups respect or admiration. This delusion of grandeur results in their views being prejudiced or intolerant toward any person of color thought to provoke negative reactions, marking the beginning process of becoming a racist.

Often, when people are prevented from succeeding in or accomplishing a goal, they generally try to determine just what happened. Reasons range from bad luck in the circumstances to intentional interference by another identity group, or an individual person working against them. If they arrive at the latter, however erroneous the assumption, reasoning may lead to conflict differences even if a group or its member was not behind the prevention. That is, faulty attributions contribute to errors in value judgment, which causes negative outcomes to occur even though its consequences could have readily been avoided.

Faulty communication is another social factor of racial conflict that appears to play an important role in racial violence. Whites in dominant society begin to see a resolution in racial conflict by imposing their values or belief systems on others. The imposition is more often interpreted as destructive criticisms. *Destructive criticisms* can leave a person in ruins or with strong feelings of retaliation by affecting his or her status among the group. These criticisms can contribute to a paradox of racial violence even though conflict does not necessarily come from incompatible interests.

A third social factor of conflict that leads to racial violence is *attribution bias* in which an individual develops the tendency to perceive his or her own views as unbiased and thoughtful while regarding other people's attitudes and opinions prejudiced and self-imposed. Those who develop this tendency will exaggerate incompatible interests by magnifying differences between their views and other people's opinions, setting the tone for racial violence. The strength of motivation often leads to *status quo bias* or the tendency for powerful interests to protect existing state of affairs through lobbying and legislating against challenging groups whose members, in contrast, have better perceptibility for intergroup relations. For instance, special interest groups tend to perceive their position as more reasonable than in actuality.

Finally, conflict amounting to racial violence has more to do with personal attributes or traits. The Type A patterned individual who is marked by impatience, aggressiveness, and competitiveness has an increased likelihood of committing violence toward opposing groups compared to the mild mannered Type B personality who never gets into a single conflict.

Might we also say racial violence is not some nonreversible or unchangeable pattern of aggression moving in a contrary direction? In fact, whether cognitive dimensions are dispositional or situational, all inevitable occurrences of racial violence can be prevented or reduced.

What Can We Do To Resolve It?

What can we do to resolve this perpetually thorny problem called racism? How can we solve its difficulty when it's complicated by various degrees, dimensions, successions, and aggressions? Each dimension has negative consequences that ultimately shape the color of our souls.

Racism is a realization born of long experience. But, there are other ways to resolve this problem. First, we need to take a look at developing an initiative to combat it. This initiative must take into consideration its core argument: the belief that various racial groups have different qualities and abilities, which mean some racial groups believe their people are inherently superior to others.

This initiative must also take into account arguments for and against its planned development. In fact, a series of events took place that created a world of hostility for Black people. From the colonization of Jamestown, Virginia to the establishment of auctions on Wall Street, racism has been the preferred method of oppression that dominant society worked out a long time ago.

Second, we need to understand that racism is a disease of the soul just like being dependent on cigarettes and alcohol. For example, most people do not consider cigarettes to be a drug because they smoke. Similarly, most people fail to consider alcohol a drug because they drink. And, the same is true for racism. Most people don't believe racism is an addition to racial violence because they are racist. For example, just when the person appears to have reframed (i.e., made a recovery) from further infliction, he or she relapses into a pattern of violence. But, unlike addition centers, there's never been a true initiative designed to combat it.

A few bills were passed into law that enforced a rule of conduct, which forbids hate crimes. But each falls grossly short as legislation and is in need of amending. Using talk sessions as therapy to prevent racism is impractical. So, that's not a viable option. In fact, it is extremely difficult to prevent or end racism. The best strategy is to minimize activities associated with it. Well, how do we follow through with that?

The idea is simple. We need to form cooperative groups. These groups will plan strategies to ensure that the constitutional rights of Black people are upheld. It needs to begin in states where citizens are allowed to propose or request the right to revise legislation by petition. It will give them a favorable position that allows an official representative to take action before a legislative body. The initiative would include improving or correcting motions, bills, or constitutions in order to elicit more desirable outcomes than in the past. It would also hold government officials accountable for the actions of their administrators as a direct consequence of inattention. This step usually begins at the local level.

In my modest understanding of it, racism will always exist so long as there are racial groups that can subjugate others. Even when physical differences are minimized among or between groups, we will still have ethnic behavior that mimics racism. Therefore, racism is a constant given the evolutions of humans. But humans will need to rise above their terrestrial state if they are to be enlightened. Although it's a long arduous process, this initiative is the best start for humanity as a whole.

Like any good initiative, it will confront racism without evasion or compromise. Unlike right-winged initiatives, it will never forget the structural differences that shape the suffering and lives of our most vulnerable. And unlike political conservatism, it will focus its involvement on the health and wellness of everyday, ordinary people from the community.

Specifically, this initiative will seek out ordinary people from the community, both supporters and members, with the fundamental aim of developing and revising laws that would deter political factions and the right-of-center from committing crimes against our most vulnerable people. In this case, it is sufficient to know that hate groups are dangerous to all people of color and that White Nationalists are members of hate groups. These groups traditionally show concern based on pseudosciences like eugenics, scientific racism, and the like.

Another goal of the initiative is to recruit effective leadership. The best way to recruit the most effective leadership is to make sure all representatives are from the community. Those who are not from the community should be heavily invested in it. Such recruitment techniques ensure that the initiative will stay grounded on issues most important to the people. Current resistance shows us there is plenty of work to be done.

This section concludes our discussion on racism and various dimensions of racial violence. In the next chapter, we will turn our attention to police brutality.

Chapter 4
How Police Brutality Awakened a Sleeping Nation

Think about how policing must have been in the early 1900's. What mental image comes to mind? Perhaps, it's a bunch of blundering cops moving clumsily through the Keystone streets of Pennsylvania as they fumble their latest police case. Now, think further back to the 1800's. Perhaps you can imagine a night watchman using a lantern to patrol the streets of a community in a sleeping town. Or perhaps, you are imaging the local sheriff riding through the streets on horseback to break up a dispute in the town saloon. Whatever your understanding of policing in early America is, remember, it is an extension of old colonial practices called law enforcement, which we adopted from England. However, there is even an earlier form of policing rooted in the traditions of law enforcement we need to consider and that is slave patrols.

First, let's not make distinctions between the North and South. All thirteen colonies participated in chattel slavery. But because the American South was exclusive in its use of slave labor, White Southerners feared that slave rebellions would disrupt economic opportunities and thus destroy the orderly progression of conducting business. As a result, White Southern slave holders formed slave patrols. The primary function of slave patrols was to enforce and correct the behavior of enslaved persons, especially "those who escaped or were viewed as defiant."

The first known slave patrols were formed in South Carolina (1704), nearly 155 years ago. These patrols ended only after the Civil War came to an end. Fast forward to the year 2020 and we continue to see the influence of slave patrols. There are distinct parallels that exist between today's law enforcement and the slave patrols of early colonial America. These "extralegal terrorization tactics" used by today's police are very much characteristic of the brutally violent history of yesterday's slave patrols.

In the new millennium, police departments do not look too different from slave patrols. For example, similarities include but are not limited to systematic surveillance, curfew enforcement, and even notions of who could become a police officer. In the past, only a few Blacks were allowed to join law enforcement. So is it true for today's Blacks who join the ranks of law enforcement; and, Black people continue to be met with resistance.

There aren't many people who would argue differently. There is not too much of a difference between the practices of today's law enforcement agencies and that of the practices implemented in early American colonies.

McGuire (in press)

Law enforcement has a peculiar history. Its customs continue to develop from practices implemented from early British colonies. In the 1960's, at the height of America's Civil Rights movement, laws were enacted to prevent Blacks from pushing back against the Establishment in Washington, DC. These laws extended special legal powers to law enforcement to maintain order over the public sector. Before then, the system of segregation kept the public in place. But with integration passing into law, dominant society was beginning to believe constant change was giving way to a reimagining of their country.

Many Whites felt that integration would create a degenerate form of higher civilization in this great nation of ours. They believed White people would have to constantly look over their shoulders in fear of crime and corruption. And with the Supreme Court ruling unanimously in favor of integration (1967), Americans would endure an even greater divide. Today, a rising tide of police brutality has created growing concern for Black lives. Some people say that today's police are operating like the slave patrols of yesterday. In fact, many people believe slave patrols never ended; they were merely given names like law enforcement and the police department.

A Rising Tide: Police
Brutality and the Growing
Concern for Black Lives

Wilmington, North Carolina police officers were recorded having a conversation about starting a new civil war. The police said they were looking forward to ridding the country of Black people. The comments used were vulgar and obscene. Shocking? Perhaps so! But, Black people have been dealing with racism and White supremacy since Whites began the hostile takeover of Africa.

Police Officer Michael Piner, Corporal Jesse Ward, and Officer James Gilmore were fired from the Wilmington Police Department. Officer Piner told other officers that Black Lives Matter protests will lead to a civil war; and, he was glad to hear it. More conversation ensued, ending with

Piner wanting to slaughter the entire race. But while the Wilmington Police Department was transparent about the officers involved, too little too late became the motto of many people. I mean, really, how transparent can you be when places like North Carolina has become the killing fields of America? And now that the government helped to militarized local police departments its, once again, open season on Black folk. Police departments are currently equipped or supplied with automatic weapons, armored vehicles, and other military resources, giving the police a military character or style.

Unfortunately, White people are just learning about the realities of racism. Apparently, they slept through the Civil Rights movement and were in denial about a few other liberation struggles. Black people, on the other hand, have been in the trenches, battling in the fight while trying to ally Whites against racism and White supremacy. Sad to say, it took about fifty years in order for Whites to understand that the threat and danger of racism is real. Even so, many Whites, more than we might consider, don't care enough to show concern. Many more are arming themselves, readying for a race war. And with an overwhelming amount of White police viewing Blacks as the enemy, they consider themselves an occupying force. That attitude is what enables them to see their situation as an "us vs. them" experience.

It's always been an "us vs. them" experience for Black people in America. The Ku Klux Klan has a monopoly on law enforcement. From guerrilla-style training camps and other military-oriented activities, the Klan have been joining the ranks of law enforcement as an American tradition. Many are card carrying Klan members. Others are Nationalists sympathizers. Still, more are right-winged loyalists. All are likely dangerous threats to the presence and existence of Black Americans.

The state of Missouri once issued "nigger hunting" licenses, allegedly. Henceforth, a common phrase often used among law enforcement was "coon hunting season," a contemptuous term used to refer to a Black person who today tends to live in urban cities. Today, the preferred term is pheasant hunting season. The term pheasant replaced coon as it is extremely disparaging and offensive.

Whites have always targeted Black people for victimization. So when police take their solemn oath to protect and serve, they view it as pledge of loyalty to their community. And that's basically what the police departments were designed to do, protect White people and their property. What they won't or will not do is protect and serve Black people in their community, viewing them as the enemy.

That White people view Blacks as their enemy is nothing new. They've made their intentions well known throughout the course of American history. And showing no compassion toward Black people in recent years, one would have to be in deep denial not to understand their plans with respect to race. Their intentions show the color of their souls.

There is an old story circulating among Free Masons and Klansman, a story about how to keep secrets safe. A Klan member asked a Master Mason, "How do I keep important information from Black people?" The Mason said, "Put it in a book." Why, asked the Klansman? "…because niggers don't read!" Now, the reason why I told you about the story is because White people have a history of keeping pertinent information from Black folk.

Throughout chattel slavery and most of segregation, the slave codes, then Black codes prohibited anyone from teaching Black people how to read, write, and function as a literate. To be literate is to achieve self-awareness. The future is grim for anyone who doesn't know their own history. How can people arrive at a prosperous future, if they have no idea how they got there? How can people prosper in life if they have no idea who paved the way before them? Knowing who we once were tells us who we are to become as every event in the circle of life repeats.

Cops promote racism in America. They're an aggressive bunch who intimidate or mistreat people of color. Most join law enforcement after completing high school. They learn to harm or intimidate people who are weaker than them in grade school. Many become accustomed or are attracted to the potential threat of violence that comes with being a police officer. And most—having little to no interaction with Black people throughout their lives—are given authority to lord it over those perceived as vulnerable. Curiously, most people of color do not have the sociopolitical support needed to help defend themselves against a state-sponsored organization that is fully endorsed by the US government. Therefore,

White police deliberately and habitually seek to harm or intimidate Blacks, the poor, and vulnerable people.

But, is racism part of the job description? How are so many racist White people joining the ranks of law enforcement without being noticed? Racism is weaved into the institutional policies that govern our nation. In this way, Whites are part of an entitlement, a system of advantage based on race.

As cops, they not only have the authority to ensure that law and order are maintained but can impact the lives of countless Black people who, by the way, they don't like. Cops discriminate against Black people because their authority is backed by institutional power. Black people, on the other hand, have to withstand the unpleasant effects of police brutality due to their vulnerable position in society. The point is Black Americans do not have the power to relegate people to levels of servility. Only White people do. With absolute power, Whites are not worried what shapes the color of their souls. In fact, most White people lost the ability to feel empathy for Black people. Hence, they lost their humanity and, in part, their soul.

We know that language is often used to help remove the humanity from White people. The less humanity one has, the easier it becomes to victimize a people. In this way, the faces of victimization can change every single day but the brutality will remain the same. Next, we will look at police brutality or the surmounting use of brute force.

Police Brutality: the
Surmounting Use of
Brute Force

Eight minutes and 46 seconds, the length of time it took for Minneapolis police to wrongfully kill 46-year-old George Floyd. The length of time quickly became a symbol and rallying cry for protesters. Mr. Floyd was unconscious and showing no signs of life as he laid on the ground while pinned beneath three police officers. One officer had his knee placed on Mr. Floyd's neck. The cause of his death was asphyxiation.

If that wasn't chilling enough, some onlookers echo out Mr. Floyd's cry "I can't breathe" as officers ignored mounting concerns. I can't breathe: Doesn't that statement sound eerily familiar to you? Mr. Floyd, Eric Garner, and seventy cases where victims used those three words gave a tragic account of innocent Black lives being taken from us. Breonna Taylor, Ahmaud Arbrey, and countless other Black victims from the younger generation were also needlessly and senselessly killed by law enforcement. Their deaths were part of an endless cycle of violence sanctioned by the United States Government.

So then, what's the problem? Candace Owens said Black people were criminal-minded. Aren't the police supposed to protect and serve? Why do so many Black people have a problem with law enforcement?

How Cops Justify the
Rise in Police Brutality

There is an overwhelming feeling of hope for people who join law enforcement. They take an oath to protect and serve. So, there is nobility in serving the public. But, therein lies the problem. What sector of the public do they protect; and, who do they serve, really? One way or another, the police are taught to look down on poor Black people.

Police officers have more acknowledged privileges than most people in America. As the police, cops adopt the values, customs, and traditions of law enforcement. In do-ing so, they learn to regard poor Black people as inferior and often treat them with contempt. So then, what of the police? Where's the humanity? How or why is it they continue to kill Black people? Well, the answer is really quite simple.

Blacks continue to die from police violence because those in law enforcement learned to justify their actions. And they justify it by removing the discomfort associated with the innocence of Black people. For instance, cops often refer to Blacks as perpetrators, criminals, and common animals, which justify their aggression toward them. In this way, it's okay for the police to develop intense feelings of dislike toward Black people. After all, aren't they worthless, inferior, or undeserving of respect? Such apathy allows for the brutal mistreatment of Black people. Again, the faces of victimization can change daily but the brutality remains the same.

If cops failed to justify their aggression toward Black people, they would experience cognitive dissonance. That is to say, the lack of consistency or compatibility between their actions or beliefs would cause sadness, grief, and despair. Instead, some cops lose the ability to feel normal. Others lose the ability to show compassionate human feelings. Still, many more cannot respond emotionally where Black people are concerned. So, where does that leave Blacks who join the ranks of police officer? You would imagine that a Black cop would have some level of empathy for their own people. Instead, their demeanor toward Black people is chilling.

The mentality of Black cops is most frightful. Many have little to no regard for the safety or wellness of their own people. For them, it's just another perp taken off the streets. They're more likely to arrest Blacks for minor infractions than their White counterparts. They are also more likely to subdue a Black suspect in defense of their White counterparts. And video coverage shows Black officers almost always participate in the unlawful arrest and murder of Blacks while in police custody. The evidence is clear. But, no statistics have been made readily available to the public. However, there is plenty of video coverage and footage on social media to support the claim.

In the case of George Floyd, for example, J. Alexander Kueng, a Black police officer, was arrested and charged with aiding and abetting in his wrongful death. Alex Kueng, as he likes to be called, was one of the three officers who actually held down Mr. Floyd on the ground as he asphyxiated and died. In another case, police officer Antonio Rodriguez, from Dade county Miami, Florida, punched a Black woman in the face, and then arrested her after she accused him of being Black. What's not apparent as the immediate incidence was officer Rodriguez came to the assistance of a fellow officer, allegedly White.

There are endless amounts of video footage readily available on social media. Each video covers Black law enforcement officers assisting in the wrongful arrest and wrongful death of Black citizens. Anyone with an undergraduate, college understanding of statistics can very well collect the data and generate valid results on the topic. My personal favorite and a preferred method for reporting on statistics is a meta-analysis.

The Growing Concern
for Black Lives

Given the increasingly visible violence by police and against Black citizens, there are growing concerns for Black lives in America. In the vanilla suburbs along the coasts and all across the Midwest in rural America, people are joining in on the fight to save Black Lives. The tragic loss of countless Black lives awakened many people in rural America. That awakening came, in part, from the continuous efforts undertaken by political and community activists. Many of them took vigorous and sometimes aggressive actions in pursuing justice for Black lives.

Despite the fear of exploitation and perpetual oppression, protesters boldly and bravely took to the streets in a collective effort for justice. They beat the streets, orchestrated countless campaigns, and pushed for change in public policy. And with the collection of new allies, more than fifty organizations from various communities, backgrounds, and political interests came together with renewed energy, and ready to articulate a common vision and agenda. And, with White people joining in on the movement for Black Lives, the momentum could be strong enough to change public opinion.

Today, White political demonstrations draw considerable criticism from conservative experts. Critics questioned whether they could change voting priorities. Like the rest of America, rural communities are changing its priorities. People understand their communities are becoming diverse. And to keep their communities safe, their attitudes about discrimination are constantly changing. Many have invested interest in multiculturalism since increasing amounts of biracial children and grandchildren are being born to families in rural areas. In fact, about twenty-one percent of the residents in rural America are people of color, increasingly Black and Hispanic.

In certain rural counties, people of color are the majority. In fact, there were historical Black communities and institutions in the Southeast and Midwest that were built for Black people by Black people. Many Black residents in Midwest industrial towns settled there in the early 1900's; and, they are a majority.

Racial injustices committed by law enforcement in rural communities were just as ramped as the ones happening in chocolate cities. The problem was their voices were being ignored or concealed from public view. Ironically, the lack of acknowledgement meant state officials felt that exposure would be damaging and somewhat embarrassing to their reputations.

Critics may question Whites and their ability to change voting priorities. But, I must point out that people are tactile by nature and have a need to depend on one another for survival. Western individualism undermines our basic needs for relatedness. I further charge that many of our problems like criminal behavior, social phobias and, even, single mother pregnancies are intensified by placing emphasis on being independent in America. In this way, I do believe that Western culture shifted too far toward individualism. My point is this: It's our humanity that draws us together regardless of people and their cultural background. People need a positive sense of self and connectedness to others. It's what enables them to develop, fully, as human beings.

As with any attempt to predict the outcome of human behavior, my theories would have distractions. So, the question proposed by critics obscures the extensive diversity and individual differences that characterizes a nation of people. Also, critics are forgetting that certain values like wisdom, mature love, and tolerance factor into every decision to change. So, as long as White people understand the true nature of a proposed problem, it's more likely they will rise to the occasion. But to answer the critics, yes, White people protesting in the movement will have enough influence to change voting priorities.

However, a better question to propose would be, "Will the change in voting priorities have enough momentum to impact an election?"

Black Liberation Struggles
and Racial Violence

Black people started out chanting no justice, no peace, to being fired up and not taking it anymore. They held their dignity by saying Black lives matter. But, it never did; so, hands up, don't shoot became an awakening as the world watched in horror the suffering and ill-effects of police brutality Black people endured here in America. Many people took to the streets, walking the line of distinction between protesting and rioting, which upset local law enforcement so much they choked Eric Garner to death and for what, selling lose cigarettes. His last words were "I can't breathe," which quickly became the official slogan to end the war waged against Black people, in an effort to end racial tensions and hostility.

Recently, people were back at it, protesting and rioting in Kenosha, Wisconsin over more social injustice. Why? Wisconsin police shot Jacob Blake in the back seven times; and, for what? What was his crime? Jacob broke up a random street fight between two women. What a way to commend any US citizen who selflessly and unabashedly performs a civic duty. And while Black people are riled to the end point of anger, Whites and Blacks alike have taken to the streets in violence on behalf of Jacob.

Donald Trump would soon ask mayors in the Midwest to bring an end to the protesting and rioting committed by the people. In turn, mayors began chastising him for instigating much of the racial violence. For example, Portland, Oregon was visited by a caravan of Trump supporters as they rallied in Clackamas County, and then drove through downtown Portland where they incited a riot. The Caravan of supporters were supported and energized by Trump who encouraged them to take action.

Many mayors felt Trump was a true danger to the democratic process. They believed that Trump's marginal behavior trivialized it. And with the country teetering on the brink of national disaster, it was time for citizens to rally around democracy. Why? It was the endless amount of racial abuse that caused serious emotional distress, trauma, and death to Black people. Not only did it affect Blacks, but it grabbed the attention of Whites and the rest of America. Mayors from all over the country hoped the people would come together in a high spirited attempt to bring an end to racial violence and bigotry once and for all.

Now, understand this democratic experiment we call America is an international investigation into the democratic process. In fact, contrary to contemporary beliefs, America is a Republic—a political system or form of government in which people elect representatives to exercise power for them. Having a Republic or Republican government— Republicans being the dominant culture—is one reason why there continues to be two separate and distinct cultural systems. Segregation, though unofficial, continue to segregate its citizens by using separate and unequal laws.

Meanwhile, in Kenosha, Wisconsin, police began targeting protesters and supporters of Black lives. Food truck and van drivers who fed protesters were often violently stopped and unlawfully detained by Wisconsin police for an average of forty-eight hours. The police were completely transparent about their motives. They arrested anyone who supported Black Lives Matter protesters as if to say, we will take down nigger lovers too! The violence directed at supporters for Black lives was unjustified; and, its intimidating effects created the threat of danger and harm. The country was truly divided with the Midwest now getting much of the attention.

A Glimmer of Hope: A Moral and Inspirational Awakening

America was lurking in the abysmal darkness of social despair. There was a profound feeling of hopelessness from dominant White society. Many felt that there was no hope for diversity in America. That American diversity meant the destruction of the White race. Coupled with the understanding that the White population continues to dwindle in size, for whatever the reason, there was an inherent fear among them that they were facing genetic annihilation. We then asked ourselves, why were racial tensions so high? For whatever reason, more Whites were dying than being born. And, this problem was producing a pathological view of reality. In fact, their pathology of race will send America spiraling into a medieval period.

America's medieval period is known by a few turns of events. American slavery, the eugenics movement, and segregation were arguably the darkest and most regrettable periods in US history. With the unofficial reestablishment of segregation, especially by enforcing separate social systems, separate and unequal laws would set America back to a period where it may never recover.

The world was watching as America faced two crises, a national crisis (with racism and White supremacy) and a global pandemic (COVID-19). Nevertheless, Whites refuse to let up off of their aggression toward Black people. And as I sat at home—myself a victim of two American crises—I felt hopeful that there might be some resolve to at least one.

For the first time in US history, Whites were taking over protesting in the fight for justice. Many Whites developed organizations that aligned with the Black Lives Matter movement to help voice concerns and build momentum for their cause. For example, Mothers Against Police Brutality (MAPB) immediately grabbed my attention. They were among the last groups to join in on the movement, adding new voices to the fight for justice.

Mothers Against Police Brutality was a united nation of multiracial and multiethnic mothers who fought for civil rights, police accountability, and policy reform. They fought and continue to fight on behalf of people who were victims of police brutality and deadly force regardless of race, color, or creed. Now that you have some background information on MAPB, I should tell you I felt a bit honored to see mothers from every walk of life fighting on the frontlines of justice, a first in global history, I do believe.

People were getting it; it was finally sinking in. It wasn't about Black people and their maladaptive behaviors; it wasn't about them being criminal-minded, either; nor was it the point that Black people were simply paranoid and making excuses to not perform. Thanks to camcorders, mobile phones, and social media, people were witnessing horrific and evil crimes being committed and not by common criminals but civil servants sworn to protect and serve.

Starting with the Rodney King beating (1991), people began to summon the courage to challenge existing powers of authority, voicing their concerns for a government that would leave American "families vulnerable to police brutality and official murder." It's almost as if mobile phone companies were doing their due diligence to equip citizens with the necessary provisions to fight back against the powers that be. And, I thank them for that!

It's been a long hard battle up hill; and, we continue to lose good people due to the government and its triable ignorance. But, we never lost momentum. We will always push forward during trying times. The only doubt present in the minds of Black folk was and continues to be how long will it take the rest of White America to change their thinking strategies? Good people are standing up! But, there are so many more who oppose change. Thus, will there ever be a time in history when we truly unite for love, peace, and tranquility?

What Can We Do To Resolve It?

To resolve the problem of police brutality, law enforcement will need to be held accountable. The problem is that the police continue to refute allegations of misconduct. For instance, many police refuse to be held accountable for the senseless killings of Blacks in America, many of whom die while in police custody. The trick is to justify police aggression by removing the discomfort related to people's innocence. Next, they relabel the people targeted in such a way that justifies their aggression toward them. These actions help to remove cognitive dissonance from their warp thinking strategies.

Network news media support the police by showing tainted news coverage that associates Black people with committing reprehensible crimes. In this way, White people are turned off to the idea of helping out Blacks. And, as media reports it, Blacks are bad people and thus undeserving of receiving a helping hand, especially from dominant society. Such misinformation expresses what it means to be Black while living in a hostile environment. But, there are growing concerns for Black lives in America.

There is a growing amount of organizations allied in protest with movements to save Black lives, for example. The official murders of largely Black Americans encouraged many organizations to take to the streets in open protest. For example, Mothers Against Police

Brutality (MAPB) was created in defense of mothers who had children who lost their lives due to state-sponsored violence.

White law enforcement officers often get riled up over tensions between their agencies and protestors. Many protestors become outraged at the police callus attitudes toward our most vulnerable. People often feel like the police need to be held accountable. Given the increasingly visible violence by police and against Black citizens, quite frankly, they should be held accountable.

In the past, I'm certain I said people should move away from protesting. Perhaps, now is a good time to say protesting is the first and last line of defense when combating injustice. There are many reasons we can use to illustrate why protesting should be first and last in the fight for justice. First, the goal of protesting is to build enough momentum to change voting priorities. When organizations take to the streets in protest, it shows there is a glimmer of hope for a moral and inspirational awakening.

Step two in the political process is to build national forums as well as hold seminars, press conferences, and peace rallies. These meetings need only be a single session or short, often one-day meeting devoted to presentations on and discussion of specialized topics like police brutality or the potential threat of a civil war ensuing. These meetings do not have to be, but usually are, at an advanced or professional level.

As a rule, all anyone really needs to do to effect change in behavior is promote adequate education or enough information.

In this chapter, we saw the problem of policing in America. There are various dimensions of brutality. But among the most dangerous dimensions are the ones sponsored by state government. In the next chapter, we will become absorbed deeply in racial hatred as we explore just how threatening it is really.

Chapter 5
Racial Hatred: How Threatening Is It Really?

Malcolm X coined the term racism (1936). His understanding of racial hatred was second to none. Yet he, like so many Black Americans before and after him, is now being called racist bigot. Wishful thinking; brother Malcolm is being judged by people, many of whom are prematurely concluding that he's now a racist without understanding the importance of his contributions to American society.

Malcolm X's career began shortly after he left prison in 1952. His reputation as an effective speaker was growing. Having dedicated his life to achieving racial equality for Blacks, Malcolm turned himself into a martyr, selflessly concerned more with the needs and wishes of other Blacks. Malcolm proceeded to speak at numerous mosques and soon became the speaker for the Nation of Islam.

He quickly experienced a powerful reaction from the White community after calling their race blonde-hair, blue-eyed devils who were "racists" against humanity, a term never before heard. Whites rejected him with increasing hatred even after he later extended his arms to embrace people from all races. His colossal misjudgment would cost him his life before it really began. Malcolm was assassinated (1965), allegedly by members of the Nation of Islam.

The plight of his existence was more than a personal tragedy for Blacks. Soon, people of all European hues would begin to discredit Malcolm using severe criticisms by America's most eminent authorities who dealt a heavy blow to his reputation. Malcolm X would not be talked about favorably in large circles for many years thereafter, neither by American Whites nor Blacks. But then, a movie producer by the name of Spike Lee would revitalize his image on big screen film, and this time his provocative and daring ideas on Black Nationalism would better serve Malcolm and the Black American experience.

McGuire (in press)

In the above article, Malcolm X was called a racist even though he coined the phrase. Is it even possible for Blacks to become racist? Who are considered racist? How can we describe racial hatred? Do people have a right to be racist? We will answer each of these important questions shortly.

Misconceptions of Antiwhite Racism

There is a misconception among Whites that Blacks can be racists. In light of what you may have already learned in your lifetime, racism strongly implies a right to discriminate. The right to discriminate is often written into the bylaws and policies that govern the internal affairs of our nation's institutions. These laws or regulations are part of an entitlement that gives White people a system of advantage. This advantage, which is based on race, is what gives White people the power to relegate Blacks to various levels of servility or place them in vulnerable positions in society. In this way, not only are Whites part of a system of advantage, they have the power to adversely impact the lives of Black people as an entire group. Therefore, White people often discriminate against Black people because their entitlement is backed by institutional power. Black people, on the other hand, have to withstand the unpleasant effects of racism due to their vulnerable position in society.

So, Whites who remain in conflict with Black people are mildly arrogant to presume Blacks would even be delegated the authority let alone given power to control or influence other people and their actions. Simply said, Black Americans cannot be racist against anyone because they have no power over people and their actions. But, they can be motivated by racial hatred.

In fact, with racial hatred, a Black person may feel intense hostility toward Whites. He or she may even have the ability to affect a White person. But at the end of the day, a Black person does not have the power to control the outcome of their lives. As for racism, let's be perfectly clear! White people can display open hatred toward you as a Black person and still have the power to adversely impact the lives of not only you, but Black people as an entire group.

The problem is Black people have unique circumstances that force them to exist in a subsequent role of racism. Anything a Black person does in American society is, at best, done in response to racism. How they behave, think, and feel is a direct result of racist interactions with White people. For the most part, Black people can only react to White racism. Why? They do not have the power to direct, shape, or otherwise influence internal affairs. When and if they do respond, it's often done by way of an officiant or during public demonstrations or by taking other civil actions. This type of interaction is true of any identity group that is subjugated. In this way, Black people's understanding of Whites is not based on inexperience or something foretold. Rather, the Black experience is based on a long, arduous history with Whites, a history that includes public demonstrations, protest marches, peace rallies, and other civil actions taken as an act of necessity. As a result of their unique experiences in America, Black people are often indifferent to the opinions and beliefs of Whites.

The majority of people understand that it is the prerogative of Whites to lessen the importance of Black folk. It enables them to dominate or take priority over their lives. When Whites are called out for their discriminatory views, they often lash out in hostility at the very people they subjugate. For example, they often attack Black people verbally and suddenly. Propaganda is systematically spread to deceive or distort the truth about the current state of affairs. The misleading publicity is enough to cause dis-belief among other identity groups that, out of social conformity, take on the social roles of those who subjugate others. These groups communicate their thoughts about Black people by calling their actions antiwhite racism. And while the term appears to be justified, it strongly implies that they fear the same exclusionary policy of racial inequality so many Whites have imposed on Black people throughout their intellectual history.

Use of the term antiwhite racism (also reverse racism or reverse discrimination) is not only improper, but it is damaging to the public image of White people. It conveys the inappropriateness of emotional and intellectual thinking formed by Whites about people of color long before having evidence of their morality or validity. It also makes abundantly clear the lack of interaction Whites have with Blacks.

So, while we can conclude antiwhite racism to be a mainstream concern, racial hatred may better mediate the thoughts, ideas, and opinions of Black folk who may have apathy or contempt for White people.

Is Racial Hatred
One-dimensional
or Multidimensional

You probably had problems thinking of racial hatred as something more than violence against Black people. Media bombards you with one-dimensional concepts of it. The government has now linked racial hatred to protest groups as a way to exacerbate its complexity. For instance, your mind constantly perceives racial hatred as a one-dimensional concept. So, it becomes an actual problem for people. Americans—who tend to have ethnocentric thinking strategies—do not have formal education on racial hatred. Why? They do not view it as a multidimensional concept. Racial hatred is a matter of racial aggression for them. All related problems that develop from it is purely culture-based and therefore not a problem of racial hatred.

I've looked at racial hatred among those who were trying to seek justice from dominant White society just to see if they have difficulty perceiving it as a one-dimensional or multidimensional concept. For instance, I found that Black people who protest aren't motivated to hate due to their unfortunate circumstances. In fact, the movement is essentially motivated by a need to achieve equality. Besides, Black people cannot exist as a function of change if they are consumed by hate.

The media, however, uses racial hatred as a tool used to scare American citizens into a theater of fantasies. Conversely, a person who views it as one-dimensional cannot provide the stimulus needed to effect change in thinking strategies. What I found is a pattern of fear among hate groups. In fact, hate motivated by fear is what helps to keep distance between Whites and Blacks in America.

People who view racial hatred as a dimension of oppression consider it a multidimensional concept. They also consider education and intellectual achievement as factors in controlling or reducing it. These people believe racial hatred is largely a problem among anyone who socially isolates themselves from the rest of society. Whites fall into this category since they tend to live in historically White communities. Their perception of racial hatred, unlike other complex human abilities, is one-dimensional.

How Racial Hatred
Impacts America

Americans are full of racial hatred. We hate anyone who fails to share our opinions about sexual preferences, the disabled, Older Americans, and even identity groups that land on the shores of America. Unfortunately, the entire system of slavery and its successor, institutionalized segregation, are known only to Black Americans. People often argue whether Black Americans find it easier to hate Whites since they've had a harder time adapting to life as a result of being oppressed.

Conversely, Blacks have always shown more tolerance toward Whites than was shown to them. Now, many Blacks appear to be growing intolerant of Whites and their listless attitudes toward equality of opportunity. Whites continue to deny access to education, fair housing opportunities, which is still a considerable problem, and public accommodations, just to name a few potent stressors in the lives of Black folk. Hate crimes like cross burnings, police abuse and sometimes killings of Black folk, as well as contemporary lynchings are taking its toll on them.

Fortunately, there are still occurrences where Whites and Blacks show a strong tolerance for one another. These short-lived moments were recently viewed by the world during a rash of violent protests over the official murders of Ahmaud Aubrey, Breonna Taylor, and George Floyd. And, the violence appears to be celebrated by European Whites. In addition, there are some Whites who protest government spending programs that would disadvantage Blacks and bring with it inequality of opportunity—tax breaks afforded to affluent Whites while no federal tax breaks for renters, many of whom are people of color, for instance.

There is a great debate in the research community over whether Black people will change their views of

Whites as they endure more and more discrimination. While it appears that Black people continue to show their humanity, how much more can they really take when Whites constantly devalue their dignity or self-worth? It may simply be that Blacks are growing weary of Whites, for instance. That is, a close inspection may reveal that Black people are beginning to express another side to their concerns. In fact, the problem is some Blacks may choose to reveal their intentions in the public sphere. That boldness is what causes White people to feel more discomfort, uneasiness, and fear. The Black idea of fundamental truth for racial equality and social justice may, in fact, be lost. It may appear favorable when Black people hold up under the kindness or compassion of humanity. But, when it comes time to show greater compassion to Whites, they may choose to regress.

However, when all is said and done, the fear is that Black people may continue to feel bitter about their unfortunate circumstances. That Whites never allowed them to improve by their own efforts; and, their failure to make good use of opportunities is potentially fueled by White people subjugating them. The result is they may be developing overt patterns of racial hatred. This realization brings with it the understanding that there can be no reasonable grounds for sympathizing with Whites over difficult cultural problems and, thus, no room for empathy.

It may also be possible that their polite way of speaking to Whites is just another means to express covert racial hatred toward the people who subjugated them.

Racial hatred has many dimensions, some more symbolic than others. How should we resolve this perpetually thorny problem? The future holds great challenges for those who seek to understand such problems. But we never really questioned when and whether a nation should stand back and do nothing. Truth of the matter is America has a violent tradition of racial hatred; and, this tradition is valued by Whites.

The Violent Tradition
of Racial Hatred

Racial hatred is a persistent and real problem to Black Americans. It causes them to suffer from indignity and low esteem. Racial hatred can be traced to the reconstruction Act (1877). And, its violent history has carried over into White America today. Despite its role in the Civil War (1865), racial hatred has an especially violent tradition among White Americans.

There is still a large body of Whites who will not openly express hatred toward Black people. But while these Whites may no longer display intense feelings, there are still certain types of hatred that occurs. Specifically, there are still various forms of cultural abuse that take place in society—speaking to Blacks in an insulting and offensive way—and, benefitting from their efforts, unjustly, while winning praise or attention by taking false credit for their achievements. We call this type of cultural abuse exploitation.

In a similar vein, parents may say to their children, "You need a real job instead of taking up art or becoming an artist," in an effort to teach their children good work ethics. In this way, parents superimpose their beliefs onto their children who, in turn, may become discouraged from trying to establish themselves as contemporary artists. Unfortunately, the parent's behavior is symptomatic of a pathology we never addressed. Thus, their attitude toward Whites is unhealthy. On the one hand, it's learned and partly adaptive because it survived throughout history. On the other hand, it's maladaptive behavior; because, it's counterproductive. For example, their children could internalize the negativity only to limit valued resources necessary for the development of a productive future. However, when people successfully adapt to their society under adverse conditions, we call it appropriate adaptation when living in a hostile environment.

Finally, there is a deprecation of culture and inflexibility among conservative Whites, as well as acknowledged feelings of separate and socially distinct experiences, that speak volumes to the problem of inequality. For example, White people tend to feel like they cannot understand the socioeconomic circumstances of Blacks, Hispanics, and vulnerable people. On the other hand, people of color believe most White people have no real world experience and will never understand their situation.

The violent tradition I describe is humiliating, emasculating, and degrading not only to Blacks who live in

America, but all people of color living in America as United States citizens. The suffering of indignity endured by Blacks, Hispanics, and the vulnerable has hardened many. The thuggish mentalities they adopt often lead them to find alternative lifestyles rather than to seek out an education or gainful employment. Once upon a time in America, the community looked out for its neighbors and cared enough to help one another. Today, Black communities no longer exist. And the me, I, individualistic mentality of people does not require a care. These effects can be seen in the abuse of police authority.

While people have made increasing efforts to reduce racial hatred in America, no real consideration was given until race-based motivated hatred in police departments received media attention all across America. While the government continues to function in denial, US citizens now feel the police should be held accountable for the official killing of Black and Hispanic Americans.

Despite certain beliefs of many people, the violent tradition of racial hatred will eventually cost Americans their dream. Too often, there is no accountability for police killings beyond what protesting brings to bear. The government more often praises law enforcement for their poor handling of a bad situation. Also, the Trump Administration's handling of the COVID-19 pandemic destroyed intergroup relations by placing identity groups at odds with one another. Trump promoted racial hatred and encouraged his supporters not to wear protective covering or practice social distancing. These social problems discourage group interaction and communication among racial groups.

The violent tradition of racial hatred is most definitely on the rise. The Trump administration has taken their stance by expressing discontent against people of color. As well, Trump supporters are physically attacking protesters. Why so? Many believe they're losing control of their country. All and all, the rise of racial hatred in America is taking its toll on everyone.

The Rise of Racial
Hatred in America

Racial hatred is steadily rising in America. For instance, White Nationalists, whose political views about equality, and Republicans' views on integration, are believed to be fueled by their hatred of Black and Hispanic people. In addition, racial hatred is ubiquitous because man has oppressed Black people as a tradition. The United States has a high incidence of racism with hate crimes steadily increasing in 2020.

However racial hatred, in and of itself, does not determine which society will have higher incidences of hate crimes. Recently, Great Britain which, at one point, appeared to be immune to racism, changed certain governmental strategies by leaving the European Union and closing its boarders to people of color. Countries like the United States followed suit by closing its boarders to Africans across the diaspora and countries considered undesirable. Their hope is that the lack of diversity that comes from denying citizenship to people of color will increase morale among people of European descent. The rate of police killings should also decrease in the years that follow.

How can we explain these undesirable changes in cultural attitudes? Whites from the older generation, those who teach racial hatred as a tradition, their commitment pressured many other identity groups to conform, thereby strengthening standardized norms of cultural abuse for people of color. For other White identity groups, conformity likely involved changes in behavioral expectations and social norms. It is unfortunate that many Whites are taught equality of opportunity. Yet, they continue to behave or think in ways that are contrary to what is socially acceptable or expected. The sad fact is White people are constantly pressured to conform.

In this way, tradition may help to explain the increase of cultural abuse that takes place in Black areas. When Whites and Blacks interact with one another, perceived differences in cultural tradition may produce conflict. Conflict tends to arouse anxiety or stress between them. It may also lead to greater oppression for Black people with regard to racial equality. For instance, at one point, Whites restricted Blacks from practicing functional literacy in America due to conflict differences in racial identity. What Whites believe to be racial equality, Blacks consider incidences of racism and worse.

If that's not anxiety arousing enough, Blacks have higher incidences of single mother pregnancies than Whites in America. This, Whites believe, comes from a weakening of religious commitment. Many Whites believe Blacks are immoral and thus dishonest people. Hence, they are unable to conform to normative expectations on valued dimensions. Whites believe immorality occurs significantly more among their people when they come into frequent contact with identity groups that are immoral and irreligious like Blacks and Hispanics. Whites believe other proof is made apparent when members of their racial group violate religious principles, then adopt liberal attitudes and urban lifestyles, and are no longer active in their church.

As of now, there are no strategies in use to help people navigate stressful transitions that influence cultural abuse or racial hatred toward people of color. Education programs that encourage unity among people, particularly for those who like to commit hate crimes, would be helpful. As for Whites who tend to promote racial hatred as a tradition, the rise of hate crimes by members of their communities may reflect how they view their beliefs and customs.

White Americans are changing the idea of culture. Blatant acts of racial hatred readily show that many Whites believe they have a right to be racist; and, it's a moral decision. In turn, Black people are beginning to understand that the need to protect themselves is real. Protection is especially important since most Black people are socially deprived and neglected by their government in real world situations.

A Right to be Racist:
A Moral Decision

We each have a right to be racist. It's a moral decision. The right to be racist depends on how a society views its beliefs and customs. The people of ancient Greece viewed all non-Greeks as barbarians. Their interpretation of foreign language and customs enabled their phraseology and vocabulary to become less barbaric. They valued physical appearance in personal beliefs and language as custom. Therefore, those who viewed foreigners differently had legal recourse to oppress them.

In addition, American attitudes toward racism reflect a tradition that has long since encouraged such acts. Morality as a sanctity of life should be protected. Today, we commit racism as if it is a great American pass-time, allowing people to use coercion and force to encourage it. Nevertheless, times and attitudes are changing along with the right to be racist; and, racism is being targeted for elimination.

The US constitution grants its citizens inalienable rights to freedom from oppression or imprisonment; yet, some people argue that this right does not apply to Blacks because their liberties are still subject to the three-fifths compromise. Most critics argue that Black people are pro-tected under the 13th, 14th, and 15th amendments. They believe that racism should be prevented at all cost, including cases that are motivated by genocide like black-on-black crime. In fact, those persons who seek to hate through racial violence should be prevented from committing racism as such acts are clearly a threat to morality.

Public support for the right to be racist seems feudal in that it is an ignoble gesture from those who feel they must, in some way, protect their own. Quite a few people feel that regardless how tragic the matter of racism, our constitutional right to be racist is an individual choice; otherwise, people would exist in communism, living without the right. Similarly, restricting the rights of Blacks while granting dominate society freedom and responsibility constitutes paternalism and is also a form of discrimination.

Particularly, in cases of extreme racism, the racist person may be affected by emotional distress. In fact, a great many people refuse to share the American dream with people of color and racism seems like a rational alternative. Even when various identity groups exist in one culture, many opt to discriminate against those who share in sameness traits. Muslims and Jews believe it is their religion that prevents them from interacting with people outside of their cultural groups, even though they are small groups in society.

Rather than being a natural response to the negative impact of societal ills, racism in the face of change, may be indicative of your more pervasive -isms to include sexism, jingoism, and communism. Perhaps we should help extreme racists cope with changing situations rather than giving them the moral decision or right to be racist.

The right to be racist has long since been abused as a moral decision. Although the government has, in some ways supported it, the right to be racist might trap otherwise socially well-adjusted people in an obligation to commit hate crimes. We have already seen how teenagers are pressured into committing violence against peers all the time as a socially approved alternative to being an outcast. We see daily how people of color discriminate against one another to gain social acceptance. It tends to be a slippery-slope we accept as rational that can lead to the ultimate downfall. Such practices make it easier for societal members to force society into practicing racism.

What Can We Do To Resolve It?

What we can do to resolve whether or not Black people can be racist is to clarify a few misconceptions about it. In this way, we gain a better understanding of how the premise works. We can also clarify some myths and misconceptions about racial hatred.

First, White people have historically displayed open hatred toward Black people. For example, after the Civil War (1865), General Nathan Bedford Forrest served as the first grand wizard of the Ku Klux Klan. During the Reconstruction Period (1866 - 1877), he and fellow Klan members conducted an eleven year massacre against Free Blacks. The massacre would begin American racism even though the word would not be coined until 1936. Thousands of Blacks would die behind its violent intentions. A special note of importance: As legend would have it, General Forrest ended the massacre in 1877. But, fact of the matter is he died in 1877 at the age of 56, which is the only reason why it ended.

Since Whites like to relegate Black people to vulnerable positions in society, they tend to openly display patterns of racial hatred. The notion that Blacks might express more overt patterns, given the right conditions, has remained to be seen.

Curiously, Blacks are more likely to show covert patterns of racial hatred toward Whites. There is a concept called, "Kill'em with kindness!" It's an effective strategy used to cause fear and doubt among anyone who might have subjugated you. The premise is simple: A person might try treating their oppressors in an extremely kind or helpful way, instead of returning an insult. Now, why would any person choose to take the high road when someone has done something rude or insensitive to offend them? Why? Well, using kindness to counter an insult tends to cause feelings of discomfort, uneasiness, or fear that a retaliatory action may someday occur, unexpectedly. Besides, because of our humanity, Blacks often believe in karma. In other words, we don't have to retaliate since what goes around comes around.

Still, there are Blacks who show open hatred toward White people. They may even hate every aspect of White people's racial identity and to the point of despise. And, that may be enough to affect the life of a White person. For example, a Black or some Blacks may cause a White person to move from their current situation. But, that's a rarity. My point is, at the end of the day, Black people do not have the power to impact the lives of White people as an entire group.

It's often conflict that is driven between Whites and Blacks as to why many White people feel they have a right to be racist. They say that being racist is a moral decision. The problem is people are often pressured to conform to societal expectations. If the majority of Whites choose to be racist, as appears to be the case, then other people may be pressured to cohere even though it may go against their better judgment. Thus, the best way to resolve this problem is to make racism unpopular.

If we can make racism not liked by, approved of, or acceptable to Americans in general, we could sway public opinion. That way, we can change the thinking strategy of dominant society. But, an action like this one is best undertaken by protest and lobbying groups.

These interest groups try to influence policy on issues like race, class, and equality of opportunity. It is often accomplished by attempting to persuade a political representative or influential person to support their cause. First, a group or groups will meet in a public area in or near a legislative building where people can gather and petition their political representatives. Next, in the political process, is for legislators to vote for or against bills and proposals. They also vote to revise or formally alter motions, bills, or constitutions. Try not to be frustrated, though. Your piece of legislation could go before a committee several times before moving on to the next step in the political process. Granted, we skipped quite a few steps, but if all goes well, you should have a new law in the designated timeframe.

So far, we discussed a various dimensions of racial hated as a way to better identify core arguments: How threatening is it really? As a result of Whites openly expressing racial hatred, Black people are abandoning their ascribed identities. Instead, many are now searching for their own identity, which we will now discuss.

Chapter 6
The Role of Ascribed Identities, Black Names, and Biracial Children

Beyond Afrocentrism, Black people are adopting their own names. What do we mean by that? Black people are using names that better characterize who they are as a whole. The process of choosing or making up your own name is called an avowed identity. When someone avows an identity, they are stating or affirming that the name chosen is right and true for them. It is their way of correcting personal, social, or cultural identities that other people place on them. Ascribed identities are often based on cultural stereotypes. Many Black people cannot compete in Western society using names based on a cultural stereotype. In this way, they cannot compete for resources while branded with an oversimplified standardized image of who they are as a person or people.

With Afrocentrism, Blacks adopt African names. Afrocentric names center on or originate from Africa or African culture. Black names in America are culture-based identities that Black people more often make up to sound legitimate. It can be made up of any one of the major languages: English, American, European, Hispanic, Arabian, African, or any combination of each. Jamal, Shaquan or Shaquana, and Laquisha are prime examples of names that sound right and true for today's Blacks.

Making up names became popular in the 1980s. Many young Blacks were turned off to the idea of following African tradition. Some were turned off to the idea of following a poor continent that had a falling or failing economy. Others were upset over the idea that Africans never fully accepted them. Still, there were other reasons why Black Americans resisted the idea of Afrocentrism, perhaps, from lack of awareness.

McGuire (in press)

Think about waking up in a hospital, having no idea who you are. You have to be integrated back into society. After years of suffering from amnesia, all of a sudden you recall your past. Only now you remember you had an entire family that was left behind. Today, you have new family, friends, and acquaintances. On the one hand, you're hurt over having lost your past. But while your present life is okay, it hasn't been the best. Society has been cruel to you; especially, since you had no idea of your true identity. The one thing you do know is you want to return to the life you once had.

Now imagine the dilemma Black people have today. They were stolen away from their former nations, forced to live life in a hostile environment. They lost physical and psychological contact with their former nations. Thus, the essential features of their culture were lost and not replaced by those of the dominant society. The result was Black people only knew the history White people ascribed to them. Then one day, after Civil Rights movements and continuous struggles, they awakened from a psychological state of identity confusion. And we wonder why they adopt separate thinking strategies. Black people are assigning names to their children that don't sound Afrocentric but are damn sure not white. To assign your children names that aren't ascribed to them is one of the first steps in developing your racial identity.

The problem with being oppressed by America is you have to rely on White people to tell you who you are. Your story, history, and culture rest with a people completely without mercy. That means they can tell you whatever they want; and, you would have to accept it as the truth.

In order to achieve a healthy and stable racial identity, you must take back control of your narrative. That often starts by reconnecting with your former countries or its people, institutions, and culture. The idea is to increase your awareness about what is going on in the world or about the latest developments taking place in your society.

It's more often negative stereotypes that hurt development toward more complete, modern social conditions. Awareness helps to reduce personal, social, or cultural characteristics that other people place on you. Establishing your racial identity is the first step to achieving self-awareness or racial consciousness.

In the next section, we will discuss the role of ascribed identity among Blacks. It is necessary to set the tone for further discussion. Afterward, we will look at the etiology hidden behind Black women and their unrelenting desire to change their children's ascribed identity.

The Role of Ascribed Identity among Blacks

Black people all over America are seeking out their true identity. Many are connecting to their heritage through African American history and beyond. They're celebrating Black foundational elders as part of it. They also live productive lives, balancing Black studies with the current affairs of today's society. In fact, nothing is unduly emphasized at the expense of the rest.

Despite their ascribed identity as minorities, many Blacks are educating themselves on issues relating to race, culture, and politics. Their productivity is said to be a natural ability to adequately cope with people in normal social situations. Curiously, their life is full of prejudice, stereotypes, and discrimination. So, Black parents often discuss the role of ascribed identity with their children at the dinner table. They ask their children about daily interactions, praise them for showing some understanding, and talk to them about the significance of coping in a hostile environment.

When a Black child is stereotyped or gets discriminated against by peers, for example, the parent quickly attempts to reconcile conflict differences to prevent further disagreement. Repeated conflicts can place a Black child at-risk, which can lead to a low self-concept. Low self-concept is associated with the internalization of ascribed identities often placed on them by their White counterparts. It is believed that ascribed identities like race, sex, and gender, influence a person's natural ability to function. Conflict differences are believed to be the reason why Blacks, in particular Black children, have lower self-concepts than Whites. The belief that you pretty much play out the hand life has dealt appears to correspond with anyone who spent a considerable amount of time living in multicultural societies.

Race, Self, and Self-concept

There is a great sense of pride that comes from developing your own identity. It's a way of correcting the lack of respect society has for the importance and value of your people or their lives, efforts, and achievements. When Black people make up names for their children, it's not only a way of removing the negativity associated with their ascribed identity but a gallant effort to restore their racial identity.

A most important progression that occurs in any era is the development of your racial identity. In fact, it forces White people to pay due attention to and refrain from violating your humanity, and thus how they should behave, think, and feel toward you and your people as a whole.

During the sixties and mid seventies, certain emphasis was placed on cultural richness and diversity. The emphasis appeared to increase self-concept for Black people who, in effect, achieved Black pride from developing a new racial identity. Black pride, as a movement that developed in response to White supremacy, encourages Black people to celebrate Black culture and embrace their African heritage. With the reemergence of the Back pride movement, also known as Black Lives Matter, Black people are reaffirming the importance of their position in society. However, there is the question of whether certain costs outweigh important benefits.

This type of pride has segregated Black people into separate and distinct communities and at a loss of social acceptance. Black Americans have, largely, inherited the city. Jews live in their own separate communities. And, Whites have retreated to the vanilla suburbs and rural America with clearly defined limits for what roles competent persons might play. Moreover, these communities are bound by common interests.

It's easy for people to develop positive self-concepts in communities that are tight-knit and supportive. Most of these communities have innovative strategies for coping with social problems. In addition, the sense of acceptance people achieve when living in their own community will give them great pride. Unfortunately, pride has no bearing on whether one will achieve respect or social acceptance among the cultural mainstream.

Although people might achieve a secure sense of self simply by belonging to a particular group, they may experience prejudices that exist outside their community. Conflicting values, morals, and behaviors largely identified as different by the cultural mainstream, can make it difficult to achieve what the cultural mainstream calls social competency. However, having pride in your own identity can diminish the burden of prejudice.

Today, people are beginning to see that Blacks have greater self-concepts than their White counterparts, even. Such positivity comes from removing identities that other people ascribed to them. Most people ascribe identities to Blacks based on someone else's stereotyped opinion of them. Consequently, Black women are choosing not to assign their children names ascribed to them. Instead, they develop names that don't sound Afrocentric but are damn sure not White. And I must say they are making quite a stir of life in doing so.

When Assigning Black
Names to Children

Have you ever heard anyone say that child's name sounds a bit ghetto? Well, that's because the mother more likely made it up. It could be a combination of both the mother's and father's name, like Rayshaun, for instance. It could also be a European name with an Afrocentric twist to it: Rasheeda, per se; or, something of the sort. But the one thing I am certain about is Black mothers from the younger generation do not or will not name their children based on an ascribed identity, especially when it arrogantly dismisses their people, their culture, or its history. But, understand their decision to assign their children names that sound Afrocentric tend to be unconscious. Or so they say! No one understands or has, at least, looked into the reasoning behind making up names. But Black people, in particular, Black women, have an insatiable desire to make up their children's names at birth.

Names like James, Brian, and Ronald sound authentically White or Eurocentric. But, Eurocentrism or Eurocentric names focus on Europe or its people, institutions, and cultures, often in a way that is arrogantly dismissive of other racial groups. Names like Juwanna, Shawanda, and Jaquan sound authentically Black. And they are! The problem is these names are not Afrocentric. Each is part of their racial identity. But, the names are very much disconnected from Africa. In fact, these names are part of a larger effort to achieve their own racial identity. Understand Black Americans love their country and wouldn't trade it for the world. They also have respect for Africa. But, they do not feel a connection to it or its people, institutions, or African culture. Perhaps, it is the lack of compassion Africans who live in America have for Black people that create a cognitive disconnection between the two identity groups.

Black people are often discriminated against because their names sound too Black; and by that, I mean beyond African or Afrocentric. In fact, this country is so hostile toward Black people their names could either land them a job or in the unemployment line. I guess the next logical question would be why do it? Why give your children names that sound unofficial, made up, or ill-contrived, especially when that society is hostile toward the people it oppressed?

I've often asked the question why make up names for your children? Every time I ask that question the answer is most always the same. Women from the younger generation (Generation Y) tell me they want their children to have names that sound unique; special, if you will. Women from my generation (Generation X) choose not to conform to cultural expectations when assigning their children names at birth. Black women try to fit their children into their understanding of what is allowed and expected of the social roles they envision for their children. That way, they can learn how to function free from the tyranny of Western imperialism. For this reason, Blacks are often assigned lower statuses.

Many Black women feel subjugated by Whites. They're hurt by the fact that Whites arrogantly refuse to apologize for their role in the oppression of Black people. Coupled with the understanding that White people like to exploit Blacks, as if it's their prerogative, I guess, in their own way, Black women are doing their part to contribute their efforts to a greater cause.

But what's the cause? Or, better yet, at what cost would a mother sacrifice her child's or children's ability to function productively in today's society? Although there are laws in place to ensure hiring discrimination doesn't disadvantage people, many times Blacks are discriminated against due to the names avowed to them at birth.

For example, names like Jamal tell an interviewer that the interviewee might be Black or, perhaps, Middle Eastern. Your zip code more often confirms it. Blacks with Eurocentric names like Rick Masters and Johnny Maverick more often receive calls during the application process. This level of discrimination is unlawful. That much is true. But, it's nonetheless a reality when you have people who are hostile toward the oppressed. The upside of this event is those who adopt Eurocentric names have appropriately adapted to life in a hostile society. The downside is appropriate adaptation when living in a hostile environment is unhealthy human behavior. How so?

Have you ever heard of the term when in Rome do as the Romans do? Well, that's not always a healthy adage to follow. When people internalize the social roles of their oppressor, they betray their principles. In America, that means accepting the fact that you will never have control over your own life without adopting their hostile mentality. And although you may not approve of or agree with their ways, for example, to adopt the mentality of your oppressor, either consciously or unconsciously, is shocking and morally unacceptable.

The problem is people often discriminate against their own people just to gain social acceptance. Well, why so? Most want no further conflict in their lives. However, it is considered an act of insanity to harm or be disloyal to yourself or your people by helping the very people who subjugated you, especially in the name of supremacy. Therefore, Black women who resist the status quo by giving their children names that sound Black believe they are forcing Whites to respect their people as a whole.

They understand that Blacks make up America's labor force. That Black people are and have been doing the jobs no one White is willing to consider. So, it becomes a strategic move to force White people to hire their children despite the White man's effort to make Black people conform in socially acceptable or expected ways. Remember, I said earlier that Whites oppressed Black people. And, they refuse to apologize for it.

Now, there was some form of apology given by Congress back in 2008 and again in 2009. What? You never heard of such an event? Well, jump onboard the bandwagon folk because most people haven't heard of it. Oddly enough, it received little coverage by the press. And, most Black Americans were unaware of it. But, some sort of effort was made and even in a way that commemorated the end of chattel slavery in the United States.

Another question that arises is how can a people be cognizant of their oppression when they appear unaware of their own actions? For example, they commit crimes. They are often illiterate. And, they walk in the image of their oppressors, mimicking their hair styles and mannerisms, apparently, in an effort to be socially accepted. Okay, let's get into the specifics of the hair coloring for an example.

I strongly believe that Black women, who dye their hair blonde, are searching for social acceptance. Even today, the hypocrisy of Blacks and blonde hair is comparable to Whites and cultural appropriation. The hypocrisy of it is how can Black people accuse White people of mocking Black fashion and mannerisms when they more often mimic White styles and behaviors?

The sad fact is there's enormous pressure for people to conform in society. So Blacks who understand they can never blend in do what they can to fit in. Remember the chapter on internalized hatred? Black people who adopt methods to fit in do so because they're actually trying to conform to society's cultural expectations, especially on valued dimensions. This means mimicking certain styles, fashions, and mannerisms just to find peace of mind.

Most times, the expectation of peace is dashed by skin color. These Blacks have skin color that is too dark. Regardless of what they do to acculturate themselves, they will never achieve acceptance among dominant society. Instead, you have those who will bleach their skin to achieve Whiteness. For example, more Black women are bleaching their skin today and at the risk of not being able to withstand natural sunlight. Michael Jackson allegedly bleached his skin in what many Black people felt was an effort to gain social acceptance. Now, I'm not going into the specifics of Michael's psyche. I summarized that point in my book, The Ignoble Paradox of man.

Still, even more Black people acculturate themselves in an effort to not only mimic their oppressors but to gain acceptance among them. I imagine many struggled with finding social acceptance. There is a growing body of Black people who today talk about breeding out melanin from their skin. Many married light skin partners in order to give birth to light skin children. There are even a few Blacks who will not breed in order to behave or think in socially acceptable or expected ways. These Blacks are threatened about living life as a profoundly dark-skinned Black person. They feel the burden of being dark-skin and choose not to bring children into the world who could potentially be born with dark skin. They also believe that any children they bare will, in some way, be genetically inferior. Thus, their souls are often in turmoil.

Others, who can pass for White, assume their identity. They take on the social roles of their oppressors, marrying White-only, a few, birthing biracial children in an effort to remove the melanin from their existence. The Blue Vein Society, for example, was a prominent or fashionable people in American culture. They often pride themselves on passing for White. They called their society blue vein because their blue veins could readily be seen through their pale skin. In fact, that's how they identified who would be accepted into their society.

These mulattos formed their own community with the goal of lightening up their gene pool. In their community, breeding with dark-skinned Blacks was never mentioned or discussed as part of their polite behavior. Their social life was an extreme way of conforming to America's cultural expectations. For them, the waning was a need to find freedom from conflict or disagreement among White people. Why? There is a real or imagined pressure to conform to the fixed standards or requirements of what it means to be American in Western society.

To be American in today's society, you must walk in the image of White people. That is to say, you must fit their image or bear in close likeness to the very people who oppressed you. It is necessary to form a positive image of you in their mind in order to accomplish this feat. First, you must be concerned about public image. Next, you will have to adopt their vernacular style of speech and mannerism.

That way, you create a mental image that is impressionable in their minds. The idea is to become less offensive to their fragile sensibilities. The hope is if enough people were to fit their image, Whites would eventually accept a few of your people into the cultural mainstream. It's not something that takes place overnight. In fact, if all goes well, it may take a few generations before your people can witness the fruit of their labor. But, that doesn't mean every Black person is interested in breeding out their melanin. In fact, many Blacks, to include those across the African diaspora, were forced into breeding out their melanin under the scientific practice of Eugenics.

Eugenics is the proposed improvement of human beings by encouraging or permitting reproduction of only those people with genetic characteristics considered acceptable. We know that thousands of fellow Aborigines were forced to breed out their melanin in an effort to strengthen the White population of Australia. This period of controlled breeding took place between the years 1910 and 1970. But, it gained momentum in the mid 1940's, when the scientific community endorsed it. Fortunately, the Eugenics movement has since been regarded with disfavor.

In this section, some people choose not to pass for White. Those who do pass often give birth to biracial children. Next, we will take a brief look at biracialism. Biracialism will be a twenty-first century concern for most of America.

The Cultural Paradox
of A Biracial American:
The Next Generation

The cultural paradox of being a biracial American brings forth some interesting problems. Looking at the next generation of biracial Americans, they will have considerably more control over how people perceive them than in past times. Nevertheless, there will be issues with love and hate that suggest a time of identity confusion. Nearly all people understand the paradox that exist between love and hate but recognize one is now in deep crisis with the-self.

The second dimension of a cultural paradox is more complex than loving your parent who may not look or sound like you. This issue is a particularly important problem among young adolescent, biracial males, especially if the parent cannot cope with often unique situations that a mixed race child might experience. Loving a parent who cannot cope with your experiences is a paradox within itself; for instance, feelings of being caught between two worldviews, between certain burdens and benefits of having a biracial family and, strengths and weaknesses of racial motivation as objective and subjective realties.

Without equivocation, being biracial has its benefits. It is true that a biracial American can be placed into roles entirely different from normative expectations. However, the more roles one must fulfill may actually enhance his or her opportunities for a greater social network support, better access to resources, and greater competence over certain persons.

Biracial Americans usually live in a state of conflict and uncertainty between two worlds, which always bring more burdens than benefits. Such beliefs are a personal bias that exploits cultural differences or how one thinks people will perceive him or her socially. Actually, this problem depends on parent-child interaction and as we have noted in the text, how they, as guardians, cope with differences in social perception. Only when a parent does an extremely poor job in coping with race-related issues does their biracial relationship become more burdensome for the teen.

This next point relates to the paradox of social interaction. Biracial Americans have a problem coping in race relations. Therefore, we must look at situational differences in terms of which relationships are perceived as burdensome, beneficial, or both. In this case, the richness of one's heritage may be perceived as burdensome or beneficial, depending on the social stratification status. This problem is one of give and take whereby the biracial American needs to get back some level of satisfaction, meaning, or feeling as a continuity or discontinuity of change in personality.

In brief, America is becoming a multicultural society. Such diversity involves understanding how a biracial American can perceive himself or herself as being caught between worldviews. Such a paradox involves learning how to see both parental heritages as mutually enriching.

What Can We Do To Resolve It?

What we can do to resolve the problem of being ascribed a racial identity is continue doing what we've been doing. We've undergone quite a few identity changes since the end of chattel slavery: boy, nigger, Negro, colored person, Black person, Afro-American, person of color, African American (with and without the hyphen) and more commonly, Black American. That's a lot of name changes just to find an appropriate identity for ourselves. Modestly, we're still searching for just the right identity. And thanks to music legend James Brown, Black American just might be our final stance.

The problem is, and has always been, having our identity ascribed to us at birth. The more prejudice found in a society the greater the chance of being ascribed a negative identity based on cultural stereotypes. Such stigmas are more often saddled with people for the remainder of their lives.

Pan-Africans are unapologetically African. They choose to Africanize their names; and, that's their take on life. But, Black Americans feel they're short-sighted, especially in their quest for complete separation from Whites. Conscious-minded African Americans tend to identify as unapologetically Black. They feel the views of Pan-Africans and Black Nationalist movements are unrealistic. It's the notion of moving into Africa for complete sovereignty that conscious-minded Blacks find unrealistic. Allow me to explain! In order to be an independent nation in mother Africa, African Americans will have to take over an independent African country, preferably a lawless nation. Other than that, should they choose to Africanize their identity, Pan-Africans will have to lose most of their current identity. And for most Black Americans, that's not a realistic option.

Unfortunately, if Blacks were to immigrate back to the motherland and settle, Africans from that nation will be absorbed and thus lose their identity in the same regards as African Americans here in America. Thus, they become a problem source for Africans much in the same regards we consider Whites. Besides, Pan-Africans are under the erroneous assumption that Africans would welcome drastic changes to their nations. We already witnessed what happened in the plans for a settlement in Liberia. We also understand and feel the disconnection between Black Americans and Africans, many of whom quickly become Westernized after they immigrate to America.

Some Black women believe that by assigning their children names that don't fit the norm, they take back control over their lives and the events that govern their future. Unfortunately, when you choose to avow your name as a racial identity, it more often goes against the norm. And that tends to be a slippery slope down the road to unemployment, poverty, even homelessness.

Now, that's not to discount the fact that there needs to be equality of opportunity to ensure no one will be discriminated against due to their avowed identity. As a matter of fact, young Black women continue to use names that avow their racial identity. And that's a good thing!

They work hard to reprove the misconceptions and misunderstandings of what social roles they and their children might rightfully play out in society. In fact, they will force society to accept them for who they are as a whole. In this way, they are applying pressure to the thinking strategies of dominant society; and, pressure leads to change. Black folk putting pressure on Whites to change is why I say the struggle to find our identity is already moving in the right direction.

A note of importance remains in this chapter: Can we as a people ever learn to accommodate those who differ in society as a whole. We do know that the development of Black pride can help to increase the self-concept of Black people. If we are to achieve equality of opportunity for each and every person, then there will need to be more positive interactions that lead to intergroup relations between distinct cultural systems.

As far as those who conform to societal expectations, they will eventually be absorbed into the larger society. Their differences will be minimized or eliminated or become integrated in this way. The result will be biracialism. Such a paradox involves learning how to see both parental heritages as mutually enriching.

In this chapter, we explored why young Black women are choosing their own racial identity. In this next chapter, we will turn our attention to young Black males and their reasoning for refusing to learn.

Chapter 7
Refusing to Learn: An Identity Crisis or a Political Stance?

There is no such thing as racial intelligence. Intelligence is universal. You will find equally intelligent and unintelligent people in every race and in every society. The problem that exists between Whites and Blacks in America may be a lack of motivation, determination, or ambition. By lacking I mean Black people may not be readily motivated to learn.

Many become frustrated at learning early on in life. They understand how poverty imposes considerable stress on their lives. Chronic life conditions like inadequate housing, dangerous neighborhoods, burdensome respons-ibilities, and economic uncertainties, coupled with the understanding that White people refuse to let Blacks compete in the job market, leaves dim hopes for a productive future for most.

The double standard in education also helps in their decision to not learn. Thus, the origins of these peculiarities stem from the notion that today's American school systems continue to be separate and unequal. The one thing these young Black men do know is they are being taught in school how to be good employees, not great leaders.

Having this new found understanding for their situation, are you beginning to understand why Black men are choosing to not learn? It's not an inability to learn. And it may not be their lack of motivation, either. In fact, it appears to be a bout of intelligence to not learn when learning comes at a disadvantage.

McGuire (in press)

Society is frustrated over the notion that young Black men in America are choosing to not educate themselves. Blacks are saying the decision to not learn is based on a need to develop their own identity. What is the truth behind their lack of motivation to learn? Is it an identity crisis that causes them to develop a fear of learning? Is it a fear of social competition that drives them to discontinue their education? Or, is it a political stance taken by a people who are tired of trying to gain acceptance while living in a hostile environment? Whatever their reasoning is for choosing to not learn, it appears to corroborate the idea that Black men, in particular, are unintelligent.

The understanding is intelligent people educate themselves. If that is true, and Black men are unmotivated to learn, then they must be unintelligent. The fact that Black men often choose to speak in Black vernacular reinforces the notion that they are unintelligent. The idea that structural differences between Black vernacular and Standard English language more than often prevents people from effectively communicating with Black men also tells people that they are unintelligible.

This reasoning is, perhaps, why we're well into the new millennium, yet, there continues to be in existence two Americas: one inherently White and the other unapologetically Black. Still, people are torn between two worlds that they so longingly wish to be one. Some Blacks are integrationists as they believe people from every walk of life should be socially accepted if that is their prerogative.

Others are hypocrites because they'd love to live in a society surrounded by Black people but boldly admit the need for better intellectual stimulation. Definitely, most Black people do not believe in cultural assimilation as they choose to not integrate themselves into the larger society so that their differences are eventually minimized or eliminated. And not many choose to become absorbed in such a way that they lose much of their own identity, either racially or ethnically.

Personally, I know what it feels like to be stripped of your identity. Having lost cultural and psychological contact with my traditional society; and, it has yet to be replaced by those of the larger dominant society, which means I am ignored and vulnerable. Here, in America, I am left in a society completely without mercy, having nowhere to turn, no one to confide in, and a society that provides me no relief or gives me nothing pleasant to consider for myself.

Quite a few Blacks are haunted by the notion of never being accepted by dominant White society. They are oddly terrified by their own appearances for not having narrow noses, straight blonde hair, and clef chins, features uncharacteristic of not only the haunted but Black people as a whole, features that, as a race, they will never possess. Yes, it's taken Black people a long time to learn how to love the skin they're in.

It's crazy to think why anyone would choose to live life in an ambivalent society, conflicted or confused because of competing views. Whites are pitted against Blacks, Blacks against Hispanics, younger generations against older generations, et cetera. But, the one thing that's certain is the cognitive disconnection that causes young Blacks to lose their desire to learn from members of the older generation.

Refusing to Learn

There is a problem among Blacks; and, it appears to be a problem of younger generations. It creates a cognitive disconnection between the opinions of one generation and another regarding their beliefs, political views, and values. This disconnection is unlike any that adversely impacts people in American society.

Now, there is always a problem when one generation refuses to learn from the previous. Some people call it idle-minded behavior. Others call it a generation gap. Still, some people simply refer to it as "not-learning." Whatever the reason for it, this refusal to learn is hardest felt among Black people.

As part of the generation gap, young Blacks are refusing to learn from members of the older generation. They're losing the desire to learn not only from older generations of family members but their foundational elders. Much of the given information helps to pave the way for future generations. For example, their foundational elders helped set forth civil rights laws that enable Blacks to function productively in society. Without their courage, commitment, and sacrifice, Blacks might still struggle to achieve voting rights. Granted, they are truly on the fringe of political life. In this way, they've felt the radical fringe of political conservatism. And, the conservative party is truly making attempts to recreate life as it was once upon a time.

For example, voter suppression is a strategy used by politicians to ensure that certain identity groups do not vote or are discouraged from voting during a public election. The government has a long history of suppressing Black people's voting rights. In fact, the march on Selma or the Selma to Montgomery marches was a series of civil rights demonstrations that took place to protect Black Americans from barriers that prevented them from voting. In this way, Black people are far removed from the center of politics or political interests.

People secure their future by fortifying their understanding of life. They cannot do this unless they're willing to learn from those who paved the way before them. Dr. Martin Luther King, Jr., Fannie Lou Hammer, and those belonging to that group, sacrificed themselves in the name of humanity so that Black people might move forward to achieve truth, justice, and the American dream. Only through their past progressions can Black people move humanity forward to become who they were meant to be considered as a whole.

There are a lot of Blacks from the younger generation who feel a certain loss of identity. They struggle to maintain it too. You can hear them attempting to maintain their identity when they meet during informal greetings. "What's up Black" is a conscious way of acknowledging one's racial identity. Or, it can be expressed in a heated argument when acknowledging one's disapproval over another Black person's personal achievements. For example, Blacks are often called sellout when striving to achieve higher education, if not called a sellout then bourgeois. Many Blacks feel like those who strive to achieve higher education or greater success have unrealistic expectations in life and are thus bourgeois. They're often characterized as conventional, conservative, or materialistic in their attitudes or viewpoints. In fact, the concept of not-learning developed much earlier, during the colonial period.

In the 16 century, the state of Virginia introduced slave codes. The slave codes were created as part of a doctrine to introduce slavery as an institution. It had a profound impact on indentured Blacks, many of whom would become enslaved indefinitely under the slave codes. First, the slave codes made it illegal to teach Blacks (indentured or enslaved) to read or write, crimes punishable by death. Later, in 1865, a reexamination of the slave codes called for the development of new laws.

Called the Black codes, many of the new laws were reassigned to include free Blacks. And so the Black codes made it illegal to educate enslaved Africans and free Blacks in the United States. It also gave birth to segregation, a doctrine that would create separate and unequal laws in the United States.

Segregation would discourage Black people from learning how to read and write. And in the South, segregation would continue the legacy of the Black codes, making it near impossible for Black people to earn a decent education. In fact, until 1967, Whites would discourage Black people from educating themselves, usually in fear of competing with each other over resources and space. In the minds of White people, Black success emasculates them. Such attitudes are the very reason why Black men view White success as feminine.

By 1970, many Blacks began adopting the beliefs of Whites, choosing to not educate themselves. Blacks would come to view education as a betrayal of personal principles. Their reasoning: It would be unintelligent for anyone to remain in a situation when repeatedly attacked, threatened, and humiliated publicly for making an effort to be socially accepted. Henceforth, the notion of not-learning is a rational response to living in a hostile environment.

In fact, not-learning is a political stance taken by a people who have been pushed to the point when something must be done or a decision has to be made. It is wise or acceptable to voluntarily withdraw one's beliefs and values from mainstream thinking, especially when in danger of being killed or injured. Moreover, Black people can preserve their dignity while they search out the relevance of their existence. In this way, searching for an identity is crucial.

Those who engage in not-learning do so as a way to maintain control over their existence in a hostile environment. One example of not-learning occurs when a Black person refuses to learn proper English. Instead, they speak in a vernacular known as Black American English. It is regarded as a language in its own right rather than as a dialect of Standard English. Black English is strongly associated with Black people who live in urban areas of society. Curiously, their refusal to learn is not simply from a fear of failure but often due to engaging in activities they consider to be White and thus feminine. Hence, many Black men reject the notion of speaking proper English.

Another example of not-learning occurs in the workplace environment. Many older Black men refuse to learn the etiquettes of typing. Typing has historically been a duty of women. Since typing continues to be associated with secretarial work, it is considered feminine to Black men. So, in not seeking out the job of secretary (i.e., not learning to type), they actually gain a sense of personal control, retain their masculinity, and thus affirm their racial identity.

On the other hand, younger generations of Black men are heavily exposed to technology. Cell phones, iPhones, and iPads are among the many items made in the sequence of typewriters. So, their attitude toward typing and secretarial work may be more contemporary.

Ironically, it is reasonable to consider any Black person insane who would choose to assimilate certain ideas and beliefs into the larger culture under the system of oppression. It is also an act of insanity to show disloyalty to one's people by assimilating the beliefs of the very people who subjugated them, especially in the name of White supremacy. In this way, the struggle to find their identity hasn't been easy.

Young Blacks often search for their identity while growing up in a hostile environment. Confronted with chronic life conditions and the overwhelming stress of oppression, they search for ways to protect their identity often by asserting their masculinity (femininity for women). The fact that dominant society calls Black manhood toxic Black masculinity tells me they are threatened by the courage and commitment of Black men. And for that reason, Black men are making a conscious effort to reject the qualities of dominant society. Public education, church, theater and drama, regardless of their mainstream qualities, young Black men are rejecting any and all success that equates to acting White, thus acting feminine.

And, as you can imagine, the act of purposely not learning is, in my opinion, a direct response to living in a hostile environment. Many Black people are well aware that they are not liked or respected largely due to their racial identity. So they choose to not follow the etiquettes and mannerisms of dominant society. Their decision to not learn, to not follow the rules of convention, and to not behave or think in socially acceptable or expected ways, may seem tacit and disabling to most people. Nonetheless, we should consider their actions as thought-provoking and calculating decisions to effectively deal with an antagonistic threat while living in a hostile environment. Their decision to not learn is, perhaps, the reason why young Black men adopted the term "real nigga."

Real nigga is a term of endearment used to express mutual affection among members of the young Black generation. It's a digression of the word Negro, which is dated and offensive. Allow me to digress. The word Negro implies that life for Black people began in the region of Nigeria and the Niger Congo, which is a gross mischaracterization of Black people. In fact, the evolution of Black people (Africans, if you will) began, simultaneously, in three separate and distinct locations in Africa. Hence, Black historians prefer to use the term Africoid or Akeloid or, perhaps, Akaloid, deriving its name from Alkebulan, the oldest known name of Africa.

The term "real nigga" is simply a means to verify someone as genuine and original rather than recognizing him or her as a byproduct of White supremacy dreams, hopes, and aspirations. Nigger is a derogatory word used to berate Black people. The fact that the term "real nigga" upsets dominant society tells me that young Black people totally understand the hypocrisy of mainstream culture and refuse to embrace it. Their attitudes or viewpoints also tell me that young Blacks have chosen to hold firm against the tyranny of oppression.

In using the term, real nigga, Black people are shaming Whites by reminding them that they are wrong for hating Black people. The constant reminders occur repeatedly in their use of the expression so White people will not forget their hateful legacy. Since Black people can use the term while White people cannot speaks volumes for their determination. Now if only they could understand the magnitude of the word regardless of how socially deviant it is in its usage, we can begin to heal.

Still, there is a serious problem that exists in Black society when each generation refuses to learn something about the history of the previous generation. In fact, starting with the baby boomers, many of its cohorts refuse to learn anything about their parents' and grandparents' generation. This cognitive disconnection exists because of the older generation's political views on race, class, and religion. Why is that a problem? George Santayana once said, "Those who forget the past are condemned to repeat it." And here we are once again! Only this time, young Black people are finding themselves in similar situations that their elders were once in and readily resolved.

Blacks are repeating the same actions undertaken by their elders in an effort to combat the discriminatory practices White people use against people of color. Well, what's wrong with that, you ask? Protesting is how people achieve change. Perhaps so! But, if young Blacks studied their history, strategically, they would better understand how to combat the situation of oppression. Instead, they are undergoing a trial-and-error process of finding satisfactory solutions. By this I mean young Black people are learning how to resolve racial inequality by experimenting with alternative methods and eliminating their failures. And, that's okay.

The problem I have with their trial-and-error method is twofold. First, the answer to resolving their problems lies within the pages of history. In fact, there is nothing in society that has not already happened, been seen, or been recorded. Hence, what we are witnessing is the cycle of life. So, look it up; read about it; and, learn from it! Black people would be further ahead in life (i.e., they could exist without undue restraints or restrictions) if they learned their history.

Second, education was a large part of African culture. If Black people would learn that fact, they would understand that their ancestors gave the world Western civilization. Africans brought with them into Europe an advanced level of development marked by complex social and political organization, as well as material, scientific, and artistic progressions, progressions that, today, we call modernization.

Did you know that Opera and classical music are both Moorish influences? That the Moors brought with them most of the classical instruments musicians use to perform in today's orchestras? Did you know? But like most things in history, that level of knowledge was taken away from Blacks when they were forced into chattel slavery. In fact, they were stripped of their identity and made to think of themselves as niggers. Understanding that they will never be accepted by Whites, young Blacks made good use of the N-word hence the modified term "real nigga." And, I get that!

I get that the term is an unexpected rejection of mainstream morals and values. I also get that it's a political posture given by a people whose backs are against the wall. But Black people cannot just lay awake and be aware of mainstream hypocrisy. They can't just refuse to embrace it, either. At least, refusing is only the first step in the political process of change, freedom, or liberty. Wildly, they must make a "conscious" effort to combat it. And that starts by fortifying their understanding of history.

Their refusal to learn is, perhaps, the reason why they use the term "stay woke" instead of "stay conscious." For young Blacks, the term "stay conscious" is dated, thus offensive. Stay woke or I'm woke is a political term that originated among young Black males in America. It derives from a Black vernacular language called Ebonics. Its common usage refers to an awareness of problems involving racial inequality and social injustice.

Now for part two of my second problem with using the trial-and-error method of achieving social change. "Stay woke" is a state of "awareness" because young Blacks do not fully understand their history. Nor do they trust the information given to them about it (which is, perhaps, why they have such a limited understanding of history). What they are cognizant of is that the White man's entire history is a lie. From Christianity and the holy wars to the current state of affairs, White people lied about their entire intellectual history. In this way, many Blacks believe that in order to cover up their lies, White people lied to Black people about their intellectual history. And, Whites lying about Black history has proven to be the case. Hence, their continued use of lying is one of the main reasons why young Black men refuse to learn. Black people just can't trust them!

Most of today's young Blacks consider their elders to be illiterate, others out of touch with important issues that affect the younger generation. Thus, if they cannot trust the information given to them by their elders, and they don't, then they sure as hell aren't going to trust information given to them by the very people who oppressed them. Hence, use of the term "stay woke" (translation: you know they're trying to keep you ignorant)."

Curiously, the term "stay conscious" or, simply, achieving "consciousness" comes out of the Black prophetic tradition. That tradition tells us why people use the term to characterize a Black person who is not only well-informed on issues of serious significance (like those who stay woke) but someone who fortified their awareness of important issues through the use of education, be it formal or informal. Conscious Black people are also willing to actively resist or oppose the government and its policies. In this way, to be a "conscious" Black man in today's society means you are intelligent, especially to a highly developed degree.

Blacks from the younger generation have to learn the importance of fortifying their awareness of life. So when they are required to learn proper etiquettes, they will understand that it is a part of the Black prophetic tradition.

A Blame Culture

Whites often feel Black people are forever blaming them for their personal short-comings. They consider it to be cruel and bitter criticism. As a blame-culture, Blacks are said to be quick at accusing Whites of creating problems for them. Unfortunately, their views erode the trust of other societies that trusted the Nation's government and its political leaders. They also reject accepted social and political values of government administrations and declare, publicly, a belief in universal acceptance. Blacks often express to Whites the need to tolerate their people without undue protest. They want White people to respect their right to integrate and their freedom of choice without interference from the US Government. They also reject accepted principles or standards of mainstream culture in the search for their avowed identity.

Politicians are supposed to provide support to their supporters, create a safe environment for them, and foster their wellness. So, when Black people place blame on political leaders, whether they are to blame or not, it is viewed as a vitriol response. Thus, when Black people take to the streets in open protest, often rallying against the government's position against the war on drugs, its political policies on crime, prison incarceration, and Jim Crow Segregation, as well as the values of dominant Whites, they are more often despised and therefore shunned by dominant society.

Conflict often develops in this way; and, dominant society will make attempts to pressure Blacks into changing their position in life. If a stance is taken, as it has been, intergroup conflict will cause the threat of danger or harm to person and property. Eventually, the conflict will come to a peak, at which point, a resolution is required. This phase of conflict is associated with state-sanctioned violence and antiblack discrimination to include mob violence, terroristic threats and or violence, lone wolf terrorist attacks, lynching, cross burnings, police abuse, and official murders. Often, but not inevitably, intergroup relations will stabilize. But it will not happen before conflict creates mental and physical health problems that suggest a time of identity confusion and uncertainty for Black people.

Conflict is often associated with people's quest to find their own identity. But refusing to embrace their ascribed identity leads to further denigration. People believe that a Black person who is confronted with acculturation can adapt to the pressures of change in four fundamental ways. Assimilation, integration, separation, and marginalization depend on how well a Black person answers two important questions. First, how important is my identity in the development of personal progress? And second, do I need to seek positive interactions with dominant society in order to function in the cultural mainstream? Unfortunately, the government's response is often to take or keep Black people away from the center of attention, influence, or power. In other words, Black people are forced into marginalization.

Black women are also tired of conforming to cultural expectations. As social outcaste, many reject the notion of social conformity. They give their children names characteristic of how they would like to be identified in the world. Names like Laquisha and Keisha are the ways they proclaim a new identity or take a stance toward publicly declaring their position in life. Further, Black women hope that they can create a new and improved lifestyle for their children, themselves, and their people.

Social Roles of Black Women

Confronting the cruelties of American culture, Black women have shown remarkable coping skills. Today, they are the most educated group in American society. Church activities and organizations like Black Lives Matters consume much of their time. But, their progress hasn't always been so.

Most of what we know about Black Women has always been one of negative imaging and misunderstanding. Many Black women have, in the past, been alienated by dominant society because their race, gender identity, and other barriers, like social status, prevented proper interaction with male dominant society. However, Black women play a crucial role in the idea of creating change.

Dominant society placed the social roles of Black women in a vulnerable position. Traditionally, the responsibility of a provider and breadwinner were more often male dominant roles given to husbands, fathers, or eldest sons. Unfortunately, Black women were required to function under extremely unfavorable circumstances.

The role of Black women has always been unimportant unless they made significant contributions to the household. Their social status didn't improve much by the Black man's standards, either. Community involvement and church affairs gave moral and intellectual benefit to Black women, benefits that stimulated their personal needs. This empowering achievement often improved their social status.

Oddly enough, regardless of their community and social status, Black women were still held in positions of low standard, the lowest in the country. Often singled and the parent of one or more children, they had inadequate health care. This happened through the kinds of jobs attained, which was not acknowledged by Social Service or in the case of domestic service, often went unreported even though it's a legal requirement.

How did they survive the rigors of societal standards? They kept close social ties with family for support, had strong work ethics, and turned to religion as a form of moral strength and guidance. The church has long been a source of strength for Black women, dating back to precolonial slavery. The church served as moral relief for Black women who were no longer allowed to practice village-based religious or social customs from their former nations. Most Black women had an almost superstitious, spiritual belief, even valuing the church over love and affection from their male companions.

Today, Black women are highly adaptive, resilient, and responsible. A long history of coping has taught them how to successfully deal with their oppressors. For example, they are leading the campaign against social injustice and racial inequality. Community involvement and church affairs gave them the moral and intellectual ability to do it and do it well. They're also using their skill-set to build platforms that challenge existing powers of authority. They instigate social change among political parties that publicly announce policies and promises when its frontrunners seek election. These policies and promises are understood to be the basis of political action when their political parties come into power. And, they're doing it in ways that many Black men have been left challenged.

What Can We Do To Resolve It?

The problem of not-learning can be resolved only if Blacks achieve full equality under the law. In order to do so, we must ensure the rights, treatment, values, and opportunities of Black people are equal to every racial group in America. It's not a matter of protesting. Nor is it necessary to be socially accepted in society though that would be nice. Equality can be achieved simply by reinforcing Amendments to the Constitution of the United States that were set forth to protect the rights and liberties of Black Americans. The problem with their current situation is that the government continues to infringe on the civil liberties of Black folk.

The Civil Rights Act of 1866 was the first federal law enacted to define citizenship and guarantee persons of African descent, born in or brought to the United States, equal protection under the law. Government officials began using broad and ambiguous terms to make its purpose vague or less clear. Today, such terms allow other minorities, like Asians, to take over the Black economy: land, rights, privileges, and activities that, rightfully, belong to and are meant for American descendants of slavery (ADOS). Therefore, we also need to make and control our own economies.

We can further resolve the problem by being efficient, cautious in our efforts, and in the building and operation of new economies. That means we should preserve, manage, and care for or protect valued resources. Once we have taken control of our resources, we can make a gradual shift from being a culture of consumers to being prudent managers of our own economy. In this way, we need a graceful economic movement.

We also need to shift our focus away from open protest to building national forums where people can discuss important matters with those who share common interests. These forums should also engage young people in public debate or allow them to express opinions in a law court or tribunal. Discussion groups will help challenge assumptions about the quality of leadership needed to carryout matters of general interest to include scrutinizing the effectiveness of prospective leadership.

If we cannot shift the focus of not-learning away from young Black men, then they will end up in a very dangerous situation. In fact, their rights will continue to be compromised if no one teaches them how to argue equal opportunity for themselves. Blacks are already second class citizens in the United States. The next step in the political process is to move them to a permanent underclass. And that's just what's happening, which is why young Black people say we need to search out our own identity. It may not be a conscious effort; but, subconsciously, they are trying to defend themselves against being pushed to a permanent underclass.

This chapter is the last of seven from my book, The Color of Our Souls: How Multigenerational Experiences Impact Our Lives. Perhaps you can look back and say you learned a lot about the current state of America or society as a whole. Many unanswered questions about intergroup relations remain, but this book does provide clues to resolving the problem of humanity. What could be more important to us all than the mission to reduce, minimize, or eliminate American racism? One of the most important themes of this book has been how racism impacts our social perceptions. Following this chapter, you will find an epilogue that focuses on critical issues about the necessary steps in the political process of protesting.

Epilogue
Step Two: In the Political Process of Protesting

Whether or not you realize it, you have a right to protest, publicly. For example, police killings appear to be supported by State government and so on. News media perpetuates police violence by persuading the public that the killings are justified due to the criminal nature of people involved. Blacks, Hispanics, and poor people are targeted often because they're the most vulnerable. Well, your right to protest is protected under the First Amendment.

The First Amendment guarantees you the right to peaceably assemble in order to address grievances. It also guarantees you freedom of speech while you peacefully assemble. In this way, learning the First Amendment is as essential to understanding your basic rights to protest given you want to be a productive member of society. Hence, this epilogue is designed to help you understand the steps needed to protest American racism.

The First Amendment (1789): Congress shall make no law respecting an establishment of religion, or prohibiting the free exercise thereof; or abridging the freedom of speech, or of the press; or the right of the people peaceably to assemble, and to petition the Government for a redress of grievances.

How to Protest against Racism

Racism is a realization born of long experience. Therefore, it is extremely difficult to prevent or end it. But, there are other ways to resolve this problem. The best strategy is to minimize activities associated with it. As a matter of fact, we need to make racism unpopular. If we can make racism not liked by, approved of, or acceptable to Americans in general, we could sway public opinion. That way, we can change the thinking strategy of dominant society. But, an action like this one is best undertaken by protesters and lobbyists.

In the past, I'm certain I said people should move away from protesting. Perhaps, now is a good time to say protesting is the first and last line of defense when fighting injustice. There are many reasons we can use to illustrate why protesting should be first and last in fighting. First, when organizations take to the streets in protest, it shows there is a glimmer of hope for a moral and inspirational awakening. Protesting brings a sudden awareness to problems most people may not know exist or be well-informed about. The more well-informed people are, the more they will begin to disinvest interest in the problem at-hand. Then the goal of protesting is to build enough momentum to change right of precedence like voting priorities.

Step two in the process is to shift focus away from open protest to building national forums as well as hold seminars, press conferences, and peace rallies. These meetings need only be a single session or short, often one-day meeting devoted to presentations on and discussions of specialized topics like police brutality or the potential threat of a civil war ensuing.

In building forums, we can engage young people in public debate or allow them to express their opinions in a law court or tribunal. Discussion groups will help challenge assumptions about the quality of leadership needed to carryout matters of general interest to include scrutinizing the effectiveness of prospective leadership.

The third step in this process is to form cooperative groups. These groups will develop a plan or strategy designed to ensure that the constitutional rights of Black people are upheld. But first, these groups need to understand that racism is a disease of the soul just like being dependent on cigarettes and alcohol. For example, most people do not consider cigarettes to be a drug because they smoke. Similarly, most people fail to consider alcohol a drug because they drink. And, the same is true for racism. Most people don't believe racism is an addition to racial violence because they are racist. For example, just when the person appears to have refrained (i.e., made a recovery) from committing hate crimes, he or she relapses. But unlike addition centers, there's never been a true initiative designed to combat it.

Cooperative groups should also take into consideration core arguments of racism. For example, the belief that various racial groups have different qualities and abilities, which mean some racial groups believe its members are inherently superior to others. In this way, the cooperative group must take into account arguments for and against racism or its planned development. In fact, what they need to know is that a series of events took place that created a world of hostility for Black people. From the colonization of Jamestown, Virginia to the establishment of auctions on Wall Street, racism has been the main method of oppression that dominant society worked out a long time ago.

Cooperative groups need to be situated in states where citizens are allowed to propose or request the right to revise legislation by petition. It will give them a favorable position that allows an official representative to take action before a legislative body. Each cooperative group would include improving or correcting motions, bills, or constitutions in order to elicit more desirable outcomes than in the past. It would also hold government officials accountable for the actions of their administrators as a direct consequence of inattention. This step, in the political process, usually begins at the local level.

The goal of cooperative groups is to influence policy on issues like racism, classism, and inequality. It is often accomplished by attempting to persuade a political representative or influential person to support a cause. Here, a group or groups will meet in a public arena in or near a legislative building where people can gather and petition their political representatives. Next, in the political process, is for legislators to vote for or against proposals. At this level, they also vote to revise or formally alter motions, bills, or constitutions.

Now, a few bills were passed into law that enforced a rule of conduct, which forbids hate crimes. But each falls grossly short as legislation and is in need of amending. So, chin up! There is plenty of work to be done. Try not to be frustrated, though. Legislation could go in front of a committee several times before moving on to the next step in the political process.

Like any good initiative, cooperative groups will confront racism without evasion or compromise. Unlike right-winged initiatives, these groups will never forget the structural differences that shape the suffering and lives of our most vulnerable. And unlike political conservatism, these groups will focus involvement on the health and wellness of everyday, ordinary people from Black areas in society.

Specifically, cooperative groups will seek out ordinary people from Black areas, both supporters and members, with the fundamental aim of developing and revising laws that will deter political factions and the right-of-center from committing crimes against our most vulnerable.

At this point, it is sufficient to know that hate groups are dangerous to all people of color and that White Nationalists are also members of hate groups. These groups traditionally show concern based on pseudosciences like eugenics, scientific racism, and the like.

Perhaps, the fundamental goal of cooperative groups is to recruit effective leadership. The best way to recruit the most effective leadership is to make sure all representatives are from the community. Those who are not from the community should be heavily invested in it. Such recruitment techniques ensure that the cooperative group will stay grounded on issues most important to the people. Current resistance shows us there is plenty of work to be done.

In my modest understanding of it, racism will always exist so long as there are racial groups that can subjugate others. Even when physical differences are minimized among or between groups, we will still have ethnic behavior that mimics racism. Therefore, racism is a constant given the evolution of humans. But humans will need to rise above their terrestrial state if they are to achieve true humanity. Although it's a long arduous process, cooperative groups are the best start for humanity as a whole.

References

Alexander, M. (2015). <u>Black Lives Matter</u>. Social Media [Online] Available: https://www.facebook.com/pages/Michelle-Alexander/168304409924191

Alexander, M. (2012). <u>The New Jim Crow: Mass Incarceration in the Age of Colorblindness</u>. New York, NY. The New Press.

Anderson, C. (2018). <u>White Rage: The Unspoken Truth of Our Nation's Divide</u>. Social Media. [Online] Available: https://www.youtube.com/watch?v=YBYUET24K1c

Anderson, C. (2019). Dr. Claud Anderson Discusses America's Race Based Society, PowerNomics + More. The Breakfast Club Power 105.1. [Online] Available: https://www.youtube.com/watch?v=fW39KOf_f04&t=3571s

Anonymous. (2020). <u>Memphis Riots of 1866</u>. Wikipedia. [Online] Available: https://en.wikipedia.org/wiki/Memphis_riots_of_1866

Anonymous. (2020). <u>Reconstruction and Its</u>

Aftermath. Library of Congress. [Online] Available: https://www.loc.gov/exhibits/african-american-odyssey/reconstruction.html

Anonymous. (2020). Oligarchy. Search Engine. [Online] Available: www.google.com

Anonymous. (2020). Slave Patrols: An Early Form of American Policing. National Law Enforcement Museum. [Online] Available: https://lawenforcementmuseum.org/2019/07/10/slave-patrols-an-early-form-of-american-policing/

Bradley, M. (1978). The Iceman Inheritance: Prehistoric Sources of Western Man's Racism, Sexism and Aggression. New York, NY: Kayode Publications LTD.

DeGruy, J. (2020). 2011 Building Bridges – Keynote. Alabama State University. Lecture [Online] Available. https://www.youtube.com/watch?v=pact4iJLlog

DeGruy, J. (2020). Black History Convocation 2020 with Dr. Joy DeGruy. Alabama State University. Lecture [Online] Available. https://www.youtube.com/watch?v=pact4iJLlog

Du Bois, W. E. B. (2014). The Souls of Black Folk.

Millennium Publications: Kindle Direct Publishing. [Online] Available: www.amazon.com

Dovidio, J. F. and Gaertner, S. L. (Eds.). (1986). Prejudice, Discrimination, and Racism. New York: Academic Press.

Early, G. (Sept. 2020). Afrocentrism. Encyclopedia Britannica. [Online] Available: https://www.britannica.com/event/Afrocentrism

Garza, A. Cullors, P. Tometi. O. (2013). Black Lives Matter. Social Movement. [Online] Available: https://blacklivesmatter.com/

Jones, J. M. (1996). Prejudice and Racism. (2nd Ed.) Columbus, OH: McGraw-Hill.

Katz, I., Wackenhut, J., and Hass, R. G. (1986). Racical Ambivalence, Value Duality, and Behavior. In J. F. Dovidio and S. L. Gaertner (Eds.), Prejudice, Discrimination, and Racism. New York: Academic Press.

Kaufman, P. (2016).Why Some Students Refuse to Learn. Blog [Online] Available: https://www.everydaysociologyblog.com/2016/01/why-some-students-refuse-to-learn.html

Linen, M. and McBride, H. (2020). I know My Rights: Bill

of Rights. Paula Chambers-Reinholdt (Ed.). Independently Published [Online] Available: https://www.amazon.com/Know-Rights-Bill/dp/B086GD6NF4/ref=sr_1_1?crid=1ND9CQT 3PZKEO&dchild=1&keywords=i+know+my+right s+bill+of+rights&qid=1604152876&sprefix=i+kno w+my+rights%2Caps%2C143&sr=8-1

Lynch M. (2020) A Guide to Ending the Crisis Among Young Black Males. [Online] Available: https://www.theedadvocate.org/guide-ending-crisis-among-young-black-males/

McGuire, B. C. (2020). The Great Divide: The Social and Cultural Context of Inequality. (First Ed.) Kindle Direct Publishing. Indie Publishing. [Online] Available: www.amazon.com

McGuire, B. C. (2019). The Ignoble Paradox of Man. (Revised Ed.) Kindle Direct Publishing, Indie Publishing. [Online] Available: www.amazon.com

Meier, K. J. (2000). Politics and the Bureaucracy: Policymaking in the Fourth Branch of Government. (4th Ed.). Orlando, Florida: Harcourt College Publishers.

Mufwene, S. S. (2020). Ebonics. Encyclopedia

Britannica. [Online] Available:
https://www.britannica.com/topic/Ebonics

Rothman, R. A. (1999). <u>Inequality and Stratification: Race, Class, and Gender</u>. (3rd Ed.). Upper Saddle River, New Jersey: Prentice Hall.

Sears, D. O. (1987). <u>Symbolic Racism</u>. In P. Kitz & D. Taylor (Eds.), Towards the Elimination of Racism: Profile in Controversy. New York: Plenum.

Schaefer, R. T. (2005). <u>Race and Ethnicity in the United States</u>. (3rd Ed.). Upper Saddle River, New Jersey: Prentice Hall.

West, C. (2008). <u>Hope on a Tightrope.</u> Carlsbad,California: SmilyBooks

West, C. (2017). <u>Race Matters</u>: Boston, Massachusetts: Beacon Press.